To my good friend Fred and his lovely wife Marilyn, with my best wishes for a healthy and happy life.

Joseph Kalina

A HOLOCAUST ODYSSEY

DEUTSCHES REICH

VORLÄUFIGER FREMDENPASS

Nr. 24619 Y/44

A HOLOCAUST ODYSSEY

Joseph S. Kalina

with Stanley R. Alten

Studies in the Shoah

Volume IX

University Press of America
Lanham • New York • London

University Press of America,® Inc.
4720 Boston Way
Lanham, Maryland 20706

3 Henrietta Street
London WC2E 8LU England

Printed in the United States of America
British Cataloging in Publication Information Available

Library of Congress Cataloging-in-Publication Data

Kalina, Joseph S.
A Holocaust odyssey / by Joseph S. Kalina with Stanley R. Alten.
p. cm. — (Studies in the Shoah ; v. 9)
1. Jews—Slovakia—Persecutions. 2. Holocaust, Jewish (1939-1945)—Slovakia—Personal narratives. 3. Kalina, Joseph S., 1917- . 4. Slovakia—Ethnic relations. I. Alten, Stanley R. II. Title. III. Series.
DS135.S55K35 1994
940.53'18'092—dc20 94–31767 CIP

ISBN 0–8191–9729–7 (cloth : alk. paper)

The paper used in this publication meets the minimum requirements of American National Standard for Information Sciences—Permanence of Paper for Printed Library Materials, ANSI Z39.48–1984.

A HOLOCAUST ODYSSEY

A Holocaust Odyssey takes place in Slovakia between 1936 and 1945. Although little has been written about events in this backwater of World War II, it was no less lethal a place than the better known killing grounds. Eighty percent of Slovakia's Jews perished in Hitler's gas chambers.

A Holocaust Odyssey is not a typical Holocaust biography. (Of course, none really is.) It is an unusual story of heroism and survival. It is the story of a Slovak Jew, Joseph Kalina, who faced certain death several times only to be saved by improbable occurrences; who felt safer in a German concentration camp than he did in his own country; who was forced to carry out ludicrous missions for the administrator of a Messerschmitt airplane factory too damaged to manufacture planes, missions that took him to Gestapo headquarters in Munich, to the Slovak consul in Vienna, and to Slovakia's second most powerful official-the rabidly anti-Semitic Interior Minister-in Bratislava.

The story is more ironic and paradoxical that it is calamitous, but it is no less riveting and compelling than stories found in archetypal Holocaust biographies. Joseph Kalina's odyssey takes the reader through the full gamut of emotions one anticipates from a survivor's tale.

For the victims of the Shoah, dead and living

and

Hedy Kornfeld Schreiber

Contents

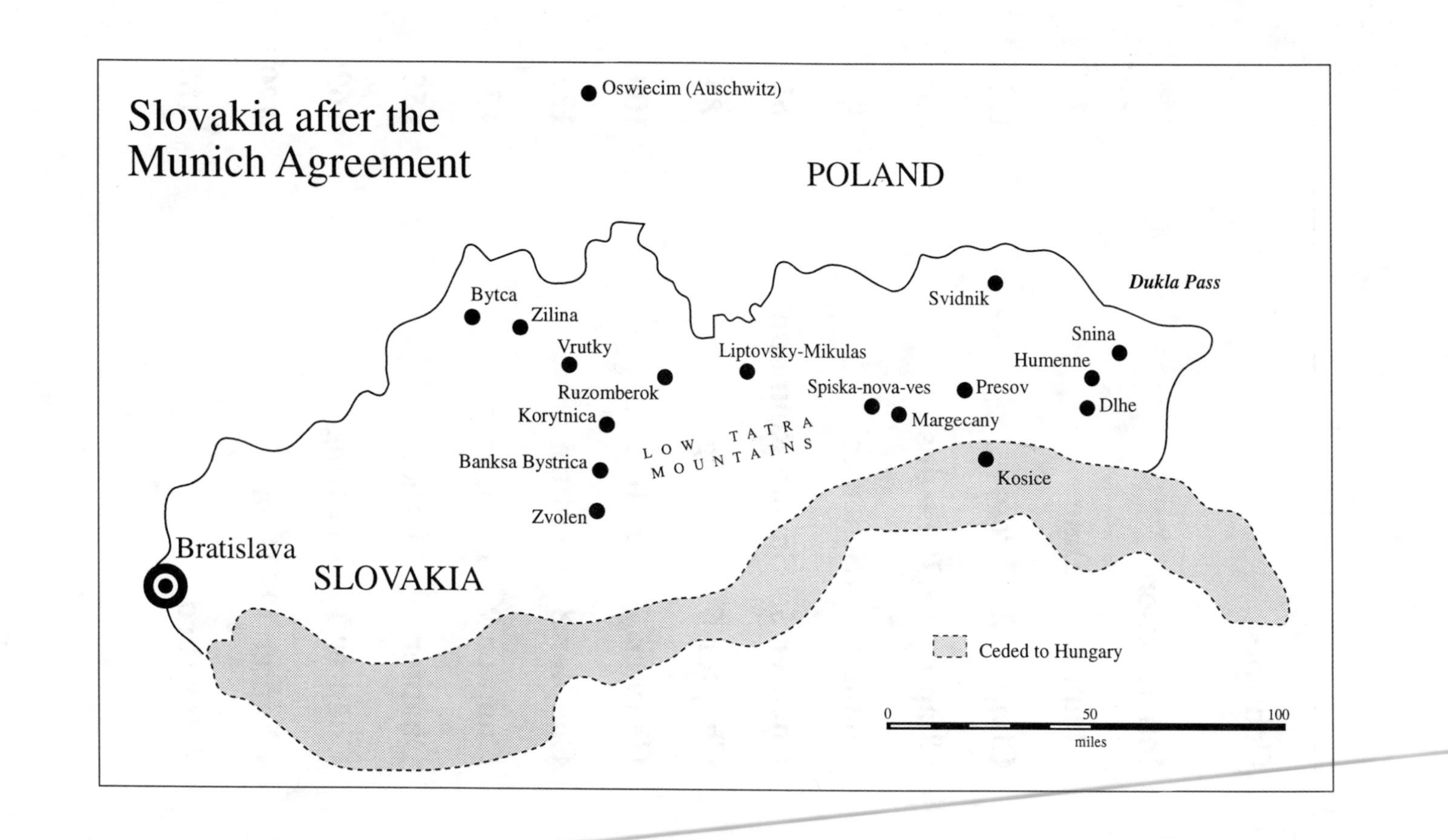
Slovakia after the
Munich Agreement
Oswiecim (Auschwitz)
POLAND
Dukla Pass
Bytca
Zilina
Vrutky
Ruzomberok
Liptovsky-Mikulas
Svidnik
Snina
Humenne
Spiska-nova-ves
Presov
Dlhe
Margecany
Korytnica
LOW TATRA
MOUNTAINS
Banksa Bystrica
Kosice
Zvolen
Bratislava
SLOVAKIA
Ceded to Hungary
0
50
100
miles

INTRODUCTION

The Holocaust is a watershed event in the history of the human race. Jews were murdered for no other reason than their birth. The killers had no more urgent task than to eradicate the Jewish presence from the face of the earth. The bystanders, for their part, were indifferent. Technological skill was applied irrespective of the harm it did to humans. Moreover, the trauma of those years continues. For the survivors, only World War II has ended; not their memories, their questions, their rage, or their hope. Although the *Shoah* remains unmastered and unmasterable, survivor testimony may prove to be the Holocaust's most enduring legacy. Bearing witness, survivors tell their stories in order to help future generations learn what happened, why it occurred, and to help sensitize their listeners so that the world will not tolerate genocide.

Joseph Kalina is a Holocaust survivor who has devoted his life to teaching the lessons indelibly imprinted on him during the *Shoah*. A forester in his native Czechoslovakia, Kalina sensitively recalls his childhood friendships, his forestry apprenticeship, and the time when his life began to change forever. In the process, he challenges the mores of contemporary society. For example, Czechoslovakian Jews were just as integrated into their society as are Jews in the American milieu. When news of Nazism's rise began filtering into his native town, most Jewish residents did not take it seriously. Nor, for that matter, did many others. Kalina's story can be read on many levels. But one of the primary lessons is a dramatic reminder that one should never take political freedom for granted.

Classified by the German oppressors as an "economically valuable Jew," Kalina was, for a time, useful to the Nazis. This was, however, short. As the murderers noose began tightening, Joe Kalina found himself without family, friends, or any other support network. A fugitive in his own land. Job-like, he asked two questions: What will happen after I die? Why do I have to die because I am Jewish? Movingly, he recounts the psychological power of Nazi tyranny. Terror and fear, he observes, cowed the Czechoslovakian people who were much more liberal than their surrounding neighbors. Further, Kalina remarks on the psychological dimension of Nazi oppression in observing that Jews themselves-constantly bombarded by propaganda-began feeling inferior. He powerfully describes his feelings of isolation and desperation amidst familiar landmarks that were no longer his own.

But this memoir is about the Jewish determination to live. Kalina recounts events that have about them the aura of biblical miracles. For instance, he visits Gestapo headquarters and emerges unscathed; a veritable Daniel in the lion's den. The instinct to survive is primal and in Joe Kalina's case overcame all else: the beatings and the terror, the constant running and the feelings of abandonment. Yet, the Holocaust has no happy endings. A far more common story is one of death and misery. Kalina is forever haunted by memories of a hot June day when his eight-year old niece, locked in a cattle car, pleaded for water. Joe was unable to help her. His sister and her entire family were murdered by the Nazis.

Joseph Kalina wrote this memoir as a two-fold scream: his own need to still scream out against the brutality of being physically beaten by the Nazis, and a scream of warning. He fervently believes that the Jewish experience bears universal resonance. In this, Kalina adheres to the Jewish tradition's commitment to remembrance and bearing witness. Kalina's witness deserves our attention. As does his commitment to seeking justice. I urge you to read this testimony.

Alan L. Berger, Director
Jewish Studies Program
Syracuse University

Chapter 1

Dlhe

I was born Jozef Kornfeld in 1917 in Dlhe, Czechoslovakia, a simple, sleepy, nineteenth century village, unaffected by either modern times or The Great War then raging. It was a small, out-of-the-way community tucked in the far eastern corner of the country, thirty miles from the nearest large city and almost 600 miles from Prague. Dlhe had no streets; a narrow main road ran down the center of the village along a brook, the Cirocha, with houses on either side. There was no industry and little culture. Almost everyone farmed. Each family owned a plot of land, growing most of its needs-wheat, corn, cabbage, potatoes-and raised a few cows to provide milk, butter, and cream. Anything left over was sold to supplement what, for most, was a meager existence.

I was the youngest of nine children. Only two sisters and a brother still lived at home by the time I was born. Esther was fourteen years older than I, Gitta, eleven years older, and David, six years older. I think I was an accident. Herman, my eldest brother, already in his early twenties, had a lumber business in Presov, a city thirty miles west of Dlhe. Louis, in his late teens, was preparing to emigrate to America where David would join him soon after schooling. Three other children by my father's first wife (he was a widower) were in their early thirties and had long since been on their own. Only one of them, my step-sister Deborah, had stayed close to the family. She lived in Dlhe with her three children.

My father had a smaller than average farm. He supplemented his income raising cattle and dealing in lumber. He worked day and night, six days a week. As an Orthodox Jew who took his God and religion with utmost seriousness, the Sabbath was inviolate. He raised his children in the same tradition.

The brunt of the household responsibilities fell to my mother, as it did to most women in those times. She put in a seven day work week, each day beginning before dawn and ending late at night. She took care of the child rearing, washing, mending, milking, food stores, and cooking. She prepared three meals almost every day of the year, except when Holy Days dictated otherwise. With only a cold cellar and no refrigeration, it wasn't possible to store food for any length of time.

Despite the hardships, my mother was a lovely, warm, caring, tolerant human being She understood the rambunctiousness of children and was often the buffer between us and my father's heavy-handed discipline. When she was compelled to crack down, it was with a sense of justice. My father was strict and tolerated little; he slapped first and asked questions after. Not to misunderstand, he loved his wife and children very much, but he was several years older than my mother and came from the old school that believed a child was guilty until proved innocent. As far as he was concerned, stricter was better. His philosophy was uncomplicated: live by God's law; work hard; provide for your family; raise your children to be respectful and obedient. Given their relentless workdays, my parents earnestly endeavored to give to us what affection they could. We knew they loved us and we felt quite secure.

Compared to most homes in Dlhe, which had only a single room that served as kitchen and bedroom, our house was sizeable. We had three rooms-a large kitchen and two bedrooms. Most houses had straw roofs and clay floors, our roof was shingled and the bedroom floors were wood. One thing that all houses in Dlhe had in common, they were bitter cold in winter, including ours. The wood-burning stoves threw little heat even when they burned all day.

As well as I can remember, I enjoyed the advantages of being the baby in the house until I was about five. I received the most attention and goodies, when they were available. I had only two "responsibilities:" playing and observing the Sabbath.

When my mother wasn't at hand to see to my needs, Esther took care of me. She was much like my mother, warm, giving, good-natured, and fun to be with. She was my favorite. Even after she married and moved away, I visited her as often as I could to enjoy her exhilarating company.

There was little sibling rivalry because, one, my parents wouldn't tolerate it and, two, because there was genuine affection among us. The family was always there for one another. The absence of sibling rivalry and my select status in the household abruptly changed with the arrival of the "orphans."

My step-sister Deborah's husband, David, was working in America. It was common in those days for men to go to the United States and work for several years until they had earned enough money to improve considerably their creature comforts when they returned home. It was easy to spot the houses where the men who had been to America lived, they were larger and more ornate.

Before Deborah's husband returned, she died of pneumonia. There was no question that my parents would take in their three children-Ethel, eight, Louis, five, and Martha, three-until David returned. Living conditions would be cramped, but Louis was my age and I was excited about the prospect of having an in-house playmate. Having Louis to play with, however, didn't quite counteract the effect of a three year old girl being in the house.

Martha quickly became the center of attention. She was cute and knew it, using her wily ways to wrap my father around her little finger. It didn't take her long to realize that this gave her the upper hand in dealings with her sister, brother, and me. She only had to cry out, "Zaide," for my father to stamp into the room and slap the first one of us he reached. There was no hearing, no chance for a defense. Even when we had company, they kvelted mostly over Martha.

Her power became vested. My father used to bring us candies wrapped in a handkerchief which had stuck to the fabric by the time he reached home. He always put Martha in charge of their distribution, instructing her to divide them equally. It isn't hard to imagine what she doled to us as our "fair" share. Not only did we receive smaller portions of the candies, but she gave us the most lint-covered pieces. We couldn't protest, for all she had to do was yell, "Zaide!" It's interesting how the benefits of power and how to use them are apparent even to the very young. But I must confess that Martha was adorable. She brought a special light into our home. The "orphans" stayed with us for eight years, until their father returned and took them to America. It would be a "lifetime" before I saw them again.

With Martha in the house and the start of my schooling a year later, I felt older. I decided no more "baby stuff" for me. I soon realized that with growing up comes new awarenesses. Getting out into the community

I sensed that Jews were different compared to the other villagers.

Education was compulsory. The village's only public school was Roman Catholic. Discrimination wasn't overt, it was more a result of daily procedures directed by Catholic protocols. Every day class started with a prayer. The two other Jews in the class and I were not allowed to stand and participate. The same thing occurred at the end of the day. It wasn't a comfortable feeling, but we accepted it. We had no choice. School holidays were Christmas, Easter, and Saints' Days. All the villagers took part in the celebrations, except the Jews. In school, there was no mention of Rosh Hashanah, Yom Kippur, Chanukah, and Passover, the holidays that fixed our calendar and defined our heritage. To observe them we either had to miss classes or celebrate at night. This told me that we were a minority living by the majority's rules. Fortunately, that's as far as differences between Jews and Gentiles in our community ever went.

The village's population of eight hundred was mostly Roman Catholic, only about fifteen of Dlhe's two hundred families were Jewish: a Gentile-to-Jew ratio of about forty-to-one. Yet, anti-Semitism was not a problem thanks to the village's friendly, liberal, humanitarian priest who, it was rumored, had fathered a son by the parish's caretaker. For some unexplained reason the woman became pregnant, no one knew by whom, but the villagers giggled good naturedly and enjoyed making a game of guessing.

The priest, called "Holy Father" by everyone, owned a handsome, open carriage unlike any in the village. When weather permitted, he took daily rides. The carriage had two seats in front where the driver sat and two seats in back where the priest and parish caretaker rode. It was coated in a rich-looking black lacquer bordered by polished bronze and pulled by a team of magnificent white horses. The priest was so well liked by the villagers that no one resented the display of opulence. Quite the contrary. Life was so hard and tedious that watching such an elegant carriage and splendid horses pass was a highlight of our day.

The caretaker's boy, Ernst, and I were classmates and became friends. Sometimes we played together after school. I remember one afternoon we were in the large kitchen of the parish house. Some breakfast bacon was still on the table. Of course he knew as a Jew I was forbidden pork products, but he wanted to tease me. He picked up the bacon and came toward me trying to force me to eat it. Naturally, I was afraid even to touch it for fear I would die. He chased me around the table shouting, "Eat it, eat it." I shouting back, "I can't, God will punish me." The priest came home in the nick of time and gave Ernst what for. When he stopped crying, the priest explained to him why Jews were not allowed to eat products from swine. I was only seven at the time but I remember how impressed I was with the priest's understanding of and sensitivity to Jewish tradition. Unfortunately, not every parish priest was so enlightened, as we soon would discover.

Another indicator that Jew and Gentile were different was the Hebrew school we had to attend before public school. I was there at five a.m. Most Gentile children were not even up at that time. I studied until seven-fifteen, ran home for breakfast, and was at my desk in public school by eight.

It wasn't bad enough having to be in Hebrew school so early, the teachers made it worse. The small Jewish community couldn't afford a full-time instructor. Each season one was hired from Humenne, a small city about ten miles away. Jewish families chipped in for his room and board. For some reason, those teachers were intoxicated with power. They badgered us, scolded us, and wrapped our knuckles for incorrect answers or the slightest suspected misbehavior. In winter, students with sleds had to take turns picking up the teacher and pulling him to Hebrew school. One day, when Louis and I had the assignment, we decided to take some revenge. We followed a route that required negotiating a small ditch. Pulling him across, we tipped the sled just enough for him to fall off and go tumbling in the snow. Of course, we acted appalled at the accident to cover our intent. It wasn't until after Hebrew school let out that we were able to slap each other on the back and roar with laughter at our small victory.

After public school ended in late afternoon, I met my friends for more work. As a group, we helped each other with the chores, one day at my house, the next day at someone else's house. We cut firewood, cleaned and restacked fireplaces, cleaned stables, and took perishables into the cold cellars, always on the lookout for goodies hidden away in pantries or holes in the wall which we filched when the mothers weren't looking. After the chores, I had dinner and did my homework. I had plenty of it; often it took me until midnight to finish.

Harvest time was worse. I rose at three in the morning and worked eighteen to twenty hours a day. Sometimes I got so weary I hid in a hayloft and slept, pulling the ladder up with me. When my father found me, which he always did, he shouted at me to come down, getting angrier and angrier because he couldn't get at me. Realizing that threats wouldn't work, he tried strategy that was transparent even to an eight year old. He calmly asked me to "please" drop the ladder, he had to come up to get something. Once he got it, I could go back to sleep. We always wound up making the same agreement: I would come down only if he promised not to punish me. So down I came and went back to the fields, but not before he managed to give me a boot on the behind with the warning not to do it again.

Arduous as life was, except for occasional lapses, I prided myself in being a good student in school and doing my chores well at home. It made me feel responsible and needed. Workdays were long and hard and existence was insular, yet our social life was comparatively active.

We usually celebrated the Sabbath with friends. On holidays, the house filled with well-wishers and we, too, made the rounds to convey greetings of Happy New Year! Happy Chanukah! Happy Passover! Sometimes, my brother Herman and his wife, Alice, came from Presov. After her marriage, Esther and her husband, Eli, made the long trip from Spiska-Nova-Ves with surprises for everyone. With the coming of each holiday I gleefully anticipated the feasting and fun. I especially looked forward to the rare treats: oranges, bananas, exotic cakes, and fruit preserves.

We also had a good time visiting Gentile families at Christmas time. Superstition had it that if a Jew came early in the morning on Christmas day to wish a Gentile a Merry Christmas and a Happy New Year, their holidays and the coming year would be blessed. Christmas morning I and several of my friends made the rounds wishing villagers seasons greetings. It was well worth it. We were rewarded generously with apples, dry fruit, and nuts.

The only problem at holiday time was the first two nights of Passover. My father conducted the seder to the letter of the scripture. Mother rigged a bedlike setting at the head of the table so he could recline during the service and meal, as was the custom. It represented the times long ago when the freeing of the Jews from Egyptian bondage was celebrated lavishly. During the seder, lying comfortably on his cushions, he fell asleep from time to time. The Haggadah was open in front of him. When he snored the pages often flipped over. No one was allowed to wake him so I would cough loudly, or David would walk around the room heavily, or Louis would plunk a dish on the table. Father would wake with a jump and re-start the seder from whatever page was showing. It was just our luck that the pages flipped backward more often than they flipped ahead. Hours later when the service finally ended, we were starving and far past the point of being thankful to Moses or for our ancestors release from bondage.

Storytelling also made life more bearable. With the absence of radio, movies, and social clubs in Dlhe, it was a favorite pastime. My parents, who read only Yiddish, recited to me the vivid tales from Jewish literature. I loved listening to the heroic exploits of my forebears. It was also exciting to listen to the tales suitors related when they came courting Esther and Gitta. They told of spirits and apparitions, some they claimed to have witnessed first-hand. Often, we younger children were not permitted to hear such frightening stories. I will never forget one tale I did manage to overhear.

There was an old school building in ruins that I had to pass every morning, usually in the dark, on my way to Hebrew school. A suitor told Esther that one night at midnight he saw a ghost on a silver carriage pulled by four white horses, with live angels sitting on it, fly out of the building. Did that frighten me! As there was no other route to school, for the longest time I had to face my fear each morning. I passed the ruins either hugging the buildings on the opposite side of the street, hiding my eyes, or running by it as fast as I could. Looking in all directions, I always feared that the ghost and his horses would fly out at me. That story's powerful effect stayed with me for years.

In most stories whenever an apparition appeared, it was always at midnight. Another hair-raising tale told of a rabbi who, one night, was crossing the river near the village in his horse-and-buggy when one of the wheels caught on the rocks. The more he whipped the horses on, the deeper the buggy mired in the rocky river bed. Some time later, at the stroke of midnight, ghosts appeared and freed the buggy. The horses virtually flew out of the river, the ghosts' presence undoubtedly providing the motivation. Thereafter, it was the prevailing wisdom among the villagers to stay clear of places where ghosts were known to be if it was necessary to be out late at night. When I happened to be awake at midnight, I was always grateful to be safely at home. Stories of the mystical and supernatural played a large part in our lives and had a decided affect on my imagination.

I had an Aunt Miriam, my father's sister-in-law, who lived in Dlhe with her married daughter, Rose. She also had a son, Avram, who was Herman's age and sold lumber in Humenne. Several years later, he would figure prominently in a scheme that could have cost me my life.

When I was about six years old, my mother was suddenly called to Aunt Miriam's house to help deliver her daughter's baby. Apparently, there was no one to take care of me so she dragged me along. My aunt's house consisted of a kitchen, bedroom, and hallway between them. I was plunked in the hallway and told to keep out of the way. Loud screams were coming from the bedroom. Women were running back and forth between the kitchen and bedroom carrying steaming cloths and pans of hot water. I thought they were killing whoever it was in the bedroom. I peeked into the room, but all I could see was a women in bed facing the wall being held down. I couldn't tell who it was. She kept screaming. I thought she was being knifed. I was shooed out of the way and had to stand in the hallway listening to her screams and watching the commotion. It was petrifying. I couldn't understand why the woman in bed was being tortured and why my mother was not doing anything to help her. No one explained to me what was actually happening and in those days children didn't ask questions. I was afraid for months. Every time I had to pass my aunt's house I felt fear and terror, believing for the longest time that it was a place where women were tortured. Even years later, when we'd visit Aunt Miriam and Rose and I knew what had taken place that terrifying day, I couldn't help glancing into the bedroom with misgiving.

Superstition also had a decided influence on our lives, often having the impact of religion itself. One day when Ernst and I were playing after school, a call came to the priest to perform last rites to a very sick woman at a nearby farmhouse. The priest usually conducted the ritual assisted by Ernst and an altar boy, one to carry the cross, the other to carry the incense canister. The priest went on to be with the woman while Ernst went to get the altar boy. He was nowhere to be found. Ernst insisted I stand in, promising that no one would recognize me in the altar boy's robe. Much against my protestations, more from fear of my father's wrath if he found out, then from God's for participating in a Catholic ritual, I was pressed into service.

At the farm house, I held the canister as the priest performed the rite. The priest didn't recognize me but the woman's husband did. To my good fortune, he remained silent.

Within the week, the farmer's wife miraculously recovered. Word spread that a Jewish boy had been one of the ministrants in the ritual. A few weeks later, another farmer needed last rites and they asked my father to let me assist. Of course, he didn't know anything about it. Well,

I don't have to describe his reaction when I came home. My career as an altar boy ended abruptly.

Unless you became a farmer, Dlhe held no future. My three brothers had left to seek their fortune elsewhere: Herman in Presov and Louis and David in America. In those days, a man was free to pursue his career. For a woman, it was different. She lived at home until she entered into her predetermined "career" of marriage and children and went to live wherever her husband settled. Esther accepted that convention. Gitta did not. Having a family was less important to her than beginning a new life in Israel. Her aspiration was unthinkable for a single girl in those times. Father adamantly opposed the move, as did all of his friends. He consulted with the rabbi who also came down in full support of my father. The standoff between Gitta and my father went on for some time, until one day she just upped and left. One of the ironies here is that Gitta, rebellious and non-conformist, disobeying my father, the rabbi and the conventions of the time, survived the war in Israel. Esther, the "good" girl, so giving and good-natured, who did what was expected of her, was deported to Poland with her family in 1942, never to return.

By the time I finished grade school, which went to roughly the equivalent of fifth grade, I was the only child still at home. Upon graduation, my parents thought they had a little genius on their hands. I was ten and they wanted me to continue my studies in high school so I could become something.

High school, or Gymnasium, was either four-years or seven-years. The seven-year schools led to a Bachelor's degree. The Gymnasium closest to Dlhe was a four year school in Humenne.

I commuted to Humenne daily by train which left at six-ten. Again, it was a time of very long days. Classes began at eight. We didn't get out of school until three, then it was back home on the train to do chores and homework. I went to high school in Humenne for only a year, still I have pleasant memories of that time, especially of my newly acquired friend, Ludovit Argay.

Ludovit and I were classmates and took an immediate liking to each other. We enjoyed the same things, particularly jokes and soccer. Our personalities were complementary: he was timid, I was outgoing; he followed, I led. We respected each other for different reasons. He admired me and I liked his enjoyable company and devoted friendship. Though we were best friends during school, after school we went our separate ways. We lived too far apart to see each other socially. He was also a Catholic. Who could have known then that our high school friendship would one day help to save my life?

I transferred to a seven-year Gymnasium in Presov. Since my brother Herman lived there, it was the likely choice. I stayed with him and his family-by then he had two children, Hedy and Paul-in their small apartment on the outskirts of the city.

After three years of Gymnasium in Presov, my brother decided the lumber business was for me. I agreed, by default. Father wanted me to became a rabbi, mother wanted me to be a lawyer. A career in forestry seemed the least of the evils. It was a fateful decision. Several years later, it helped save my life.

The closest forestry school was in Humenne, so back I went to Dlhe to live with my parents and for the next three years commute five interminable days a week. The only relief from studies and from chores was getting together once in a while in Humenne with my old school chum, Ludovit Argay, and fishing with Ernst, the caretaker's son. On rare occasions, my parents and eight or ten of their friends rented a horse and buggy and we went to Snina to see a Jewish play. Snina was the equivalent of the county seat. The shows were simple morality plays performed by a touring company, but they were a welcome diversion from the rigors of work and undeviating routine.

Difficult though my studies were, they were greatly rewarding. Forestry school provided me with a solid theoretical education in wood technology. I learned the entire process from seedling to living room: planting, growing, structure, pathology, processing, utilization.

After graduation, I wanted to complete my studies at the university in Prague. To qualify, university rules required a two year apprenticeship in a professional lumber operation. Once again I returned to Presov, this time to work full time for my brother. It was stimulating to be back in the city and exhilarating to have finally left the insular life of Dlhe behind, especially now that my career was assured and the future looked so bright. It was 1936.

the knowledge. The theoretical raw material that I learned in school had to be forged in the crucible of experience before it did me much good.

And did I make mistakes! Oak cut down instead of cherry, maple instead of elm, wrong measurements, incorrect tallies. And did my brother chew me out! In his early counsel, Herman had tried to prevent me from making a fool of myself, but in the young there's often more immaturity than even the best of intentions can redirect. It took a while.

Young I may have been, but dense I wasn't. In time, I learned my business well and Herman became satisfied with my work. He gave me a promotion, a raise, a new suit, and a motorcycle. He also gave me increasing responsibility in dealing with customers.

Schooling had not only taught me foreign languages, it had refined the languages I already spoke. I was able to converse in German and Hungarian without a Slovak accent and I could speak Slovak without a Yiddish accent. Since most of our business was conducted in those languages, the added polish gave me a decided advantage in the business world, especially during the war when Germans accounted for eighty percent of our trade. Herman, on the other hand, had a heavy accent. He spoke mostly Yiddish growing up and had not gone beyond grade school. He also tended to be emotional; I was more detached. My appearance was another reason Herman wanted me to work with clients. I was tall and well-built and he seemed to think I presented a more refined demeanor; he was short and stocky. However, his native intelligence, inherent kindness, and fearlessness made him unsurpassed as a brother, friend, and businessman.

Now I was a big shot. I had a terrific job that paid well, more responsibility in the business, dressed in style, and zipped around town on my new motorcycle.

Coincidentally, my social life picked up.

At first, it was difficult adjusting to my new life. Though I had lived in Presov before, it hadn't been long enough to think of myself as other than a small-town boy. Except for a few former schoolmates who travelled in other circles, I knew no one. I was also bashful about girls. Regardless, Alice thought it was time I started to think about settling down.

She introduced me to neighbors with children my age who introduced me to their friends. Word got around that Joe was a nice guy and a good catch. Soon I became part of a clique: David Sekely, who became my best friend and roommate, owned a photography store next door to our company's office; Fritz was a radio mechanic; George worked in a foundry; Saul sold paper products; Susan was a school teacher; and Edith and Monica led the conventional lives of most single women. Once they graduated high school, they helped around the house cooking, sewing, knitting, and waiting for marriage.

I had a crush on Susan, a striking, well endowed, young woman. Unfortunately, she cared for George. She tried to ease the awkward situation by introducing me to her friend Maria Markovic. In due time, we became sweet on each other and Maria became part of the group. She was tall, a bit plump, with chestnut hair, and light brown eyes. Though she wore glasses to correct nearsightedness, they didn't take away from her attractiveness. People said we made a good-looking couple. Not to be immodest, I agreed. I was fairly good looking-six feet, one inch tall, 180 pounds, with brown hair, gray eyes, and agreeable non-defining features, including a high forehead, a sign of intelligence, I was told.

Because almost everyone worked long hours during the week, social activities were limited to weekends. Promenading along Presov's main streets was a popular pastime. It was strictly against social etiquette for a young person to advance him- or herself to someone before being introduced. That made it difficult to meet any one outside of your immediate group of friends. Promenades provided the opportunity to scrutinize members of the opposite sex and show off at the same time. If you spotted someone of interest, it was up to you to make arrangements to be introduced.

Even when you were going with someone, social mores and the ever present chaperon made it difficult to be alone together. Maria and I may have been a couple but going on a date by ourselves was out of the question. We saw each other only when our clique got together.

Summer weekends we hiked through the beautiful, secluded woodlands that dotted the area, or went to the nearby resort to eat wurstel-a Czechoslovakian hot dog-or bathed in the mineral springs close to the resort. When we could, some of us took out-of-the-way routes to neck. They were about the only opportunities I had to be alone with Maria and the closest we came to intimacy. Although given our physical relationship, "intimacy" is too strong a word.

In winter, the group went to the movies, to the theater, kibitzed, and had parties Sunday afternoons. When we weren't partying, a few of the boys and I went to the Jewish Community Center to play Gin Rummy for money. The stakes were modest, we couldn't afford to lose much. We got together mostly for the company and for the food and drinks that were put out.

When he was in town, I saw my old school chum from Humenne, Ludovit Argay. He was a travelling salesman and on the road most of the time. He had moved to Presov with his parents who were school teachers. When it became risky for Gentiles to be seen with Jews, we saw little of each other socially, but his sympathy for the Jews' plight remained ardent and our friendship stayed strong.

On major holidays, family came together. Either my parents travelled to Presov, or Herman, his family, and I went to Dlhe. Sometimes, Esther, her husband, and two children joined us, making the long journey from Spiska-Nova-Ves. The trips to Dlhe were a particular delight, not only because it meant a family reunion, but because our friend, the priest, always had his magnificent carriage waiting for us at the train station. The ride to my parents' home reminded me how, as a child, a highlight of my day was seeing the priest, the parish caretaker sitting by his side, take his daily carriage ride through the village. We were, of course, grateful for his kindness whenever we came to Dlhe, which we appreciated even more so, in hindsight. Dlhe's parish priest was among a breed of cleric soon to become rare in my country.

In 1938, with my apprenticeship over, I was eligible to continue forestry studies at the university in Prague. I had become excellent at my work, made a good salary, and had a wonderful social life. Though I was going with Maria, word still had it that I was a good catch. When I returned from the woods in the evening, one or two girls were usually hanging around outside the office. It was good for the ego, though I have to confess that sometimes I didn't know whether I was the attraction or it was my motorcycle. Regardless, I was diffident with women. I always had been.

On a business trip the year before, I sat on the train across from a woman who was so stunning I had all I could do to keep from staring at her. Given the proprieties of the time, speaking to her without an introduction was out of the question. Besides, she was obviously older than I.

I was going to Kosice, a city twenty five miles south of Presov. Rail service being what it was, I had to change trains in Kysak, a village smaller than Dlhe, twenty miles west of Presov. Upon arriving at Kysak, the station master informed us that because our train was late, the connecting train had already left. The next connecting train wasn't due until five the next morning. The woman, half a dozen other passengers, and I were stranded for the night.

The small inn close by-the only one in the village-had only half a dozen rooms and was full. Serendipitously, the inn keeper was my old playmate from Dlhe, Ernst, the parish caretaker's son. He told me to wait in what he called the lobby and he'd see what he could do. The lobby was a small room, dark and chilly, with two threadbare chairs. The lady was sitting there when I walked in. I don't know where the other passengers had gone. Our mutual problem helped break the ice and we struck up a conversation. She was a Hungarian aristocrat, married, on her way to visit family in Kosice. Ernst came in and said I could have his room for the night, it had a couch and a bed. He had to be on duty until six. I proposed to the woman that she take the room, that I could manage on the chair in the lobby. She politely declined saying that the inn keeper was my friend and it wouldn't be fair of her to do so. I volunteered to stay in the lobby with her to keep her company for the night. We made light conversation for a while. Finally, I said that to sit here like this made no sense. I suggested that we both take the room. She could have the bed, I'd sleep on the couch. She agreed to share the room but only on the condition that I make her a promise to behave as a gentleman. I gave her my solemn word. She went to the room first, undressed, and was in bed when I walked in. Seeing her lying there so tempting and vulnerable, the cover framing her ample bosom, was almost more than I could endure. But I took my promise as a gentleman seriously. Quietly, I laid down on the couch, desperately trying to think about anything to take my mind off the ravishing lady just a few feet away. It took me a long time to fall asleep. We had to get up by four thirty to catch our connecting train. We agreed that who ever woke first would wake the other. When I got up the next morning, she was gone and so was her bag. I dashed out of the room to see if she was in the bathroom at the end of the hall. It was empty. I had overslept! It was when I returned to the room that I saw the note: "This is what you deserve for being a gentleman." Obviously, I had missed much more than a train connection that morning.

I came to Presov, a peasant from the country, to be a big shot in the big city. I brought with me the youthful afflictions of immaturity, inexperience, and naivete; an enervating combination of attributes if left unattended. But I persevered and felt I was well on my way to becoming an authentic "know-it-all-guy." I was having a good time.

We were aware from radio and newspaper reports that the Germans were being provocative and annoying. They blamed the Allies, the Bolsheviks, and the Jews in particular, for rubbing the Fatherland's face in the ruinous Treaty of Versailles with which Germany was forced to comply after the Great War. They also railed about the Sudetenland rightfully belonging to them. Germans were a petulant people and Germany was far enough away; their grievances didn't seem to have much to do with Czechoslovakia.

As it is with so much in life that we can neither anticipate nor account for, I hadn't the slightest notion that the following year the world as I knew it would begin to disappear. That my bright future would become a fearful daily struggle for survival.

Chapter 3

It Begins

In November 1938, against Czechoslovakia's vehement cry to the world of rape, the Allies gave the Sudetenland to Germany. On March 14, 1939, Germany decided to dismember Czechoslovakia. The western half, Czech, or Bohemia as it was also called, became a German Protectorate. Since the Germans took the better part of the country, with its industry and raw materials, they were generous with the rest, undoubtedly because they knew they would get it back soon anyway. Poland was given a piece of the country's northern region; Russia annexed a chunk of the east; and Hungary took a small slice of territory in the south. What was left became the "independent" state of Slovakia.

After all these years, it's still difficult to understand how a group of supposedly civilized leaders of state-except for Hitler, of course-representing modern, industrial, nations could agree to take a sovereign country and, by fiat, write it out of existence, utterly indifferent to the wishes and welfare of its people.

With Czechoslovakia dismembered, its rail, road, telephone, and telegraph communications were disrupted. The Germans appropriated seventy to eighty percent of its iron and steel, electric power, textile, chemical, and coal industries. But sixty percent of the lumber industry was unaffected. Most mills were in Slovakia, and Presov was well within its borders.

When Slovakia was created it was understood that the new country would ally politically with Germany. The presence of so many German nationals in Slovakia generated strong pro-German influence making the Slovak affiliation a fait accompli.

Hitler hand-picked a Catholic priest, Monsignor Dr. Jozef Tiso, head of the Hlinka Slovak People's Party, and notorious anti-Semite, as president. When the government organized in Bratislava, the capital, it included a new branch of the Interior Ministry, the Department of Jewish Affairs. With its creation, the campaign against Slovak Jews began. The first sign of trouble was the demonstrations.

After World War I, not everyone accepted the marriage of Bohemia and Slovakia that begat Czechoslovakia. A movement of Slovak nationalists, led by a jingoistic priest, Andrej Hlinka, vigorously campaigned for a political divorce to make Slovakia independent once again.

Hlinka organized a personal, paramilitary guard modeled after Hitler's SS, on which he depended both for protection and fierce loyalty to his cause. He didn't live to see the realization of his crusade (he died in 1938), but the new government gave the now designated Hlinka Guard official recognition in his honor and named the ruling party after him. The Hlinka Guard became an elite police organization unconditionally loyal to the government and its policies, especially those involving the Jews. Their transition from body guard to state guard was relatively easy, Hlinka also had been an anti-Semite. The Guard organized a cell in every Slovak community and became the Tiso regime's bullyboys.

To impress the Nazis and help cement its alliance

with Germany, which seemed the sure winner in the inevitable war that was coming, Tiso sanctioned the Guard to begin demonstrations against the Jews. They marched throughout Slovakia with signs exhorting the people to demand their country be Judenrein-cleansed of Jews. As they marched, they sang:

> Cut and hack into the Jewish head,
> Until the blood runs out and the kike is dead.

As the demonstrations intensified, we grew increasingly more anxious. It puzzled us why the authorities permitted such malicious anti-Semitic rallies. What did the demonstrations portend? What would come next? It wasn't long until we found out.

Before Hungary took possession of the Slovak territory ceded to it with the dismemberment of Czechoslovakia, the area was temporarily declared an "open zone." Any Slovak living there, who wanted to remain a Slovak citizen, was given thirty days to move north, within the redrawn Slovak border. During the moratorium, traffic between the open zone and Slovakia would be permitted to flow freely. Once the thirty days expired, the open zone would become Hungarian and the border between Slovakia and Hungary would close.

As further proof of his "good will" toward Germany, Tiso decided to ship a few thousand prominent Slovak Jews south to the no-man's land. There they would be dumped and left to fend for themselves. Once the moratorium expired, they would become Hungary's problem. The roundup lasted only a few days, but it was long enough to ensnare Herman and his family.

It was late spring 1939. I came home from work early one evening, opened the door to my brother's apartment, and standing there was a gendarme, rifle slung over his shoulder with bayonet fixed. "What do you want?" he asked curtly, with a derisive emphasis on "you." My stomach knotted. Something was obviously wrong but I didn't know what.

"I'd like to see Mr. Kornfeld," I replied, surprised at how quickly I thought of a response. Another gendarme inside called out, "You can't see Kornfeld now, he's tied up." I thought to myself, "literally or figuratively?" He sounded friendlier than the gendarme at the door. The way he studied me I could tell he knew I was connected with the family in some way. I saw Alice sitting on the sofa crying and moved toward her. The second gendarme put up his hand, "I said Mr. Kornfeld is busy right now, so why don't you go like a good boy and not interfere." Whatever the reason, he had decided to let me go, ignoring who I might be. Another gendarme, perhaps the one at the door, might not have been so charitable. Thus, I had my first experience with capricious lady luck. During the next six years I would have many more such experiences in which my survival would depend completely upon others and events utterly out of my control would shape my destiny.

I went downstairs to the office, stunned. When I told the staff what had happened they became agitated. For all Slovaks, Gentiles and Jews alike, it was a time of upheaval and tension. The Republic's breakup had angered everyone. The fledgling Slovak government, struggling to organize, was in disarray. It was trying to deal with the mad rush of Slovaks coming from the open zone. Czech nationals were fleeing from Slovakia to Bohemia rather than live in a country with a people for whom they had a natural enmity. And now prominent Slovak Jews were being randomly picked up and dumped in a no-man's land that soon would become part of Hungary. The instabilities brought daily life to a virtual standstill.

I had no idea where my brother's family had been taken, nor did anyone else. I phoned the Judenrat-the Jewish Council of Elders-and was assured they would try to find out, meantime I'd have to be patient. I was too anxious to sit still, let alone be patient. Thank goodness I had the distraction of a business to run. I was temporarily in charge of Lignum Lumber.

Two days later the Judenrat called with news. The afternoon Herman and his family were taken without warning or legal sanction, they were loaded into an open truck crammed with dozens of other randomly selected, equally baffled, frightened Jews. They were driven to Kosice, a bustling city of one hundred twenty thousand, which had belonged to Czechoslovakia and, for the time being, was located in the open zone. Kosice became the dumping ground for the victims of President Tiso's "good will" gesture toward the Nazis.

Though it was a relief to know where my brother and his family were and that they were unharmed, I anguished about getting them back to Presov. Once the thirty day moratorium expired and Kosice became Hungarian, they would be trapped behind the Hungarian border. I knew what had to be done, I just didn't know how to go about doing it. The next day Sessi Ritterstein arrived.

Sessi was a close friend of Alice's, going back to their early school days. She worked for a Slovak insurance company, managing its Kosice branch, which her firm had closed to beat the thirty day deadline. Like many of her countrymen, who neither spoke Hungarian nor wanted to become a Hungarian citizen, she chose to return to Slovakia. She was assigned to the company's office in Presov. Needing somewhere to stay temporarily, she had turned to her girlhood friend. I told her she was welcome to stay in the apartment until she got settled. When I explained why there was plenty of room, she was flabbergasted. In a matter of hours we began conspiring to get my brother's family back to Presov.

In Kosice, Sessi, who was quite attractive, was seeing a Slovak Army captain. As the Army was feverishly evacuating men and materiel to meet the moratorium deadline, he was making daily trips between Kosice and Presov. With thousands of Slovaks in a panic, dismantling homes and offices, taking with them what they could, rushing to get across the border before it closed, and hundreds of Jews going in the opposite direction, being summarily jettisoned into no-man's land, it was just possible in all the chaos that the family could be smuggled back to Presov. There was also another urgency in moving quickly. Their resources were limited. They had been permitted to take with them only fifty crowns-about seven dollars-and one suitcase, per person. The first two priorities were to find out where they were living, then to get them some money.

Sessi's officer friend found them staying with a business acquaintance Herman made when the company did some work in Kosice. Through Sessi and her captain we were then able to send him money and messages.

We made arrangements to smuggle Herman, Alice, Hedy, and Paul in an army truck and eagerly anticipated their arrival. Days passed. Nothing. The captain told Sessi there would be a delay. The truck he planned to use for the operation was too small to hide six people. He needed time to arrange for a larger vehicle. Six people? The news baffled me. Who were the other two?

It was my turn to be flabbergasted. They were my mother and father. Herman and I had no idea they had been taken in the roundup, let alone that they were in Kosice. The Judenrat in Kosice, which kept track of such things, had informed Herman. Three weeks after their forced departure, and just days before the border closed, a large Slovak Army truck rolled into Presov packed with military cargo under which were hidden my brother, his wife, his two children, and my parents.

The Army officer, who was not Jewish, took considerable risk to please his lady. But above that, his commendable action and courage demonstrated two things: that not everyone was hostile toward the Jews or approved of the government's anti-Semitic policy; and that having connections was crucial. As we were to learn, the right connections often meant the difference between life and death.

My family's ordeal lasted only three weeks. At the time, they were among the relatively few Jews to have made it home so soon after being taken. They were considered luckiest. Most victims of the roundup were either trapped in Hungary when the border closed, and had a difficult time returning to Slovakia, or chose to remain and become Hungarian citizens. The irony of history proved the last group to be the most fortunate. While all but a few of those who had returned to Slovakia were being consumed in the fire, the Jews of Hungary lived protected for most of the war. Against Germany's most emphatic protests, the Regent of Hungary, Miklos Horthy, stood up to the Nazis, refusing to surrender even one Hungarian Jew. He was able to frustrate the Nazi's enormous pressure until 1944 when Adolf Eichmann took personal control of Hungary's flagrant, too long neglected, "Jewish problem." Even so, by war's end, comparatively few Hungarian Jews had been "relocated." As things turned out, Herman and his family would have been better off had they stayed in Kosice.

The trauma of the family's displacement should have provided ample forewarning of events to come. Alice was one of the few people perceptive enough to sense that harder times were ahead for the Jews. Yet, there was no question of the family's returning to Presov. It's a paradox of human nature when danger threatens and common sense dictates it's time to flee your home, it takes greater courage to uproot-leave everything you've worked for to face the unknown in a strange place-than it does to gamble, waiting optimistically, albeit, in harm's way, in the hope that things get better. You buoy your spirits with dark, droll, humor. "Smile," you tell yourself, "things could get worse. So I smiled and sure enough things got worse." Whatever the pretense, you delay uprooting. With your very life in peril, deracination is extremely difficult for a human being.

Our family reunion was tearful and joyous. Alice insisted Sessi stay with us until she found an apartment. She became just like a member of the family. To make room for her, I was relegated to sleeping on a cot in the office's conference room downstairs. As our plight worsened, Sessi continued to provide both moral support and influence in high places, even after she moved to her own apartment.

Celebration of our family's safe return was short-lived. The government launched the first organized phase in its campaign against the Jews. It was the beginning of an ingenious five-phase plan to eliminate Slovak Jewry. Phase One, mark us. Phase Two, demoralize us. Phase Three, restrict us. Phase Four, starve us. Phase Five, liquidate us.

By law, a Jew now had to wear a yellow arm band on the left coat sleeve. At first, Jews wore the arm band with dignity and defiance. It was our badge of honor proclaiming: if you want to single us out, then here we are and we're proud of it! We will not be humiliated because of our religion!

Our initial reaction was untempered by fear. We figured the arm-band law was another token gesture to the Nazis in the Tiso regime's campaign of impression. Once the Nazis duly noted the new sanction, the harassment was sure to relent. After all, Jews in eastern Europe had endured persecutions many times throughout history, some escalating into bloody pogroms, others amounting to little more than disruptive inconveniences. This was just another wave of anti-Semitism and like the others, it too would pass. Hope, the anesthetizer of reason, had a willing clientele and soon addiction became epidemic. To anyone able to withstand hope's narcosis, and there were precious few, the warning signs were clear that this time, "it too" would not pass.

Every day, propaganda in newspapers and on radio decried the Jewish blot on the new Slovak nation. The populace was told of the Jews' heinous offenses against the state; of their demonic religious rituals; of their parasitic tentacles affixed to the nation's economy to suck it dry; of the opprobrium that all civilized people shared with Slovakia for history's lepers. The government made it palpably clear that Jews weren't needed or wanted in the new nation, or anywhere else.

Gradually, the effects of discrimination became demoralizing. I began to wonder if something really was wrong with us after all; if, indeed, ours was a minority in the degrading sense of the term? I recalled that uneasy feeling in public school in Dlhe when I realized that Jews, somehow, were different and life was centered around Gentiles. In Dlhe though, we were separate but equal. Now we were separate but unequal, and inferior. In Dlhe we were part of society, now we were being methodically isolated from it.

Walking along the street was an embarrassment. The yellow arm band was easy to see and all the more conspicuous because Jews were such a small part of Presov's population. People glanced at my coat sleeve and shunned me. Even close Gentile friends, like Ludovit Argay, were reluctant to be seen with me in public fearing guilt by association and later on, as a result, perhaps trouble with the authorities. The propaganda was having its effect on the population and on me.

Whenever possible I avoided going into public. When I couldn't avoid it, I took off my jacket to hide the arm band. Any Jew caught without the arm band or purposely trying to hide it was subject to a fine or arrest, or both. Though harsher punishments were still a few years away, at the time, fine or arrest were severe enough. It was late spring and so many Jews purposely walked around coatless that authorities had difficulty enforcing the law. So a new law was passed.

Instead of an arm band, Jews had to wear a yellow Star of David, ten centimeters in diameter, firmly affixed to the outer garment. The star had to be visible at all times. Even a baby in a carriage or a crib had to wear the star day and night. Now it was impossible to hide being a Jew, unless you were willing to chance punishment.

A gendarme or Hlinka Guard could stop any citizen anytime and ask for his Identification Card. It had been law in most European countries that everyone had to register for an I.D. card and carry it at all times. On the card was your picture and other identifying information, including religion. Soon, the I.D.s of Jews would be stamped with a large "J." If you were not wearing the star and were stopped, the I.D. gave you away. Then the consequences were the most severe allowed by law, including a good beating if a Hlinka Guard caught you. At the time, we had no idea that being marked by the star would become tantamount to a death decree.

Restrictions came systematically, one every month

or so. To notify the citizenry, each new restriction was posted on public bulletin boards and kiosks located throughout the city. The ominous sign that another difficulty had befallen us was the presence of a crowd surrounding a kiosk in the early morning. Jews and Gentiles crowded in to see what the government had devised. With the yellow star "firmly affixed" to our clothing, Jews read as marked men. Once marked, the next phase of restrictions-economic deprivation and physical isolation-was easier to enforce.

When war broke out in September 1939, the worsening conditions accelerated for the Jews. One morning in early fall, crowds gathered at kiosks to read the first notice in the government's campaign to limit our livelihood. It was in two sections. Part One decreed that all Jews must work but they could earn no more than one thousand crowns per month-about seventy dollars; they could be paid less, but not more. This affected eighty percent of the Jews. Part Two took care of the other twenty percent. It decreed that all Jewish businesses had to become Aryanized. A Jew had to turn over forty-nine percent of his business to a Gentile, or Aryanator, as he was called. The Gentile could be of the Jew's choosing, with government approval. However, the government could preempt the choice and appoint a Hlinka Party member or political crony. Those two restrictions constituted the first decisive step to jugulate Jewish existence in Slovakia.

It was irrelevant that an Aryanator know anything about the business he joined. In most cases, he sat around doing nothing while earning forty-nine percent of the profits.

For my brother, who had worked so hard to build Lignum Lumber, it was a daunting blow. Yet, as it is with most troubles, when everyone throws theirs into the street you're happy to pick up your own. He was able to choose a long time employee, Jan Malik, as his new partner. Malik could barely read and write but he was affable and a timber expert. He readily agreed to the partnership with the understanding that it would be in name only. Herman and I would continue running Malik and Company, as the business was now called. Like many Slovaks, Malik had no quarrel with the Jews nor did he approve of the official vendetta against us. He was, nonetheless, more than happy with the arrangement: an increase in income with no increase in responsibility.

The routine of daily life assumed a degree of normalcy, despite the intensifying difficulties. We adjusted to the restrictions, learning how to live with them. Most of us had no other choice, there was no way out.

Until fall 1939, most European Jewry could have fled to safety. Germany and its allies were only too willing to let the Jews go, sans money and possessions, of course. It was the easiest way to make Europe Judenrein. After war broke out, although communications with the west grew increasingly difficult, it was still possible for most Jews, except those in Poland, to flee. Once the Wannsee Conference laid out the blueprint for the Holocaust in January 1942, all routes out of Europe slammed shut and Nazi gas chambers and ovens went into full operation.

When it was still possible for Jews to leave Europe, most of the world community didn't want them. Countries made various excuses: they were still in the Depression and had to take appropriate measures to ensure their people had first-chance to fill available jobs; their economy couldn't accommodate large numbers of refugees due to the Depression; their immigration laws couldn't be changed nor could they adjust the quotas. Regardless of the excuses, the root cause in most instances was anti-Semitism.

The United States had lowered its immigration

barriers slightly in 1938 but began raising them again in fall 1939. Quotas for European Jewry emigrating to the U.S. were meager and, at that, they were never filled. Jews with the best chance to reach America had to have parents or children already living there. My brothers, Louis and David, had been in the U.S. several years. That made my parents eligible to immigrate. Herman, his family, and I were stuck.

A few countries, such as Cuba and the Dominican Republic, were willing to accept Jews, but you had to have the right connections and sufficient money for bribes. Hard as Herman tried, he couldn't make contact with the proper Cuban or Dominican officials.

My brothers in America, aware of the worsening situation in Europe, had the foresight to send the required immigration affidavits to our parents. We decided Mother and Father would be better off staying in Presov until arrangements for their immigration were made. The closer they were, the better we could see to their needs. We found them a place near Herman's apartment, liquidated their property in Dlhe and settled them in Presov to await their departure for America. That was the last time any of us saw Dlhe and the home of our childhood.

Herman began making arrangements for my parents' immigration the end of August 1939. The first step was to register the affidavits my brothers had sent from America with the U.S. consul in Bratislava.

The consul studied the documents, said everything was in order and officially registered them. He told my parents the next steps were to obtain their passports and visas for travel through Germany and France. The boat they'd be taking departed from Le Havre.

Herman asked the consul if I could accompany my parents? He pleaded that they were elderly and needed my assistance for their arduous trip to and adjustment in

America. The consul said I could but needed permission from Slovak authorities waiving my military obligation. All physically fit males, once they reached age sixteen, had to serve two years in the army at some time. The consul said to return once all the necessary documents were obtained. Then dates for our journey would be set.

It took more than three months to gather the official papers. The bureaucracy had to be involved each step of the way: to process, check, and recheck my parents' passports and visas; to methodically register every item they were taking with them. Herman also had to find and bribe the right officials for the military exemption.

During that time, I paid a visit to my sister Esther in Spiska-Nova-Ves. Infrequent though the visits were, I looked forward to them with a particular delight. Eli, Esther's husband, always made me feel welcome. My sister, as usual, was wonderful company. During those difficult days, she never failed to lift my spirits. I enjoyed playing with her two children, Judy and Alfred, a little younger than Hedy and Paul, but no less bright and beautiful. Judy had the same endearing personality and mannerisms as her mother.

On that visit, Esther showed me a letter she received from Gitta in Israel. It warned that things in Europe would be getting much worse for the Jews and to try and get out. Gitta had sent such letters before, but none had the strong warning and urgency of that one. When Esther and her family had the chance to leave they thought, as did most Jews, that times would get better and they'd wait it out. Now, for them, as it was for Herman and his family, it was too late.

We returned to the American consul in December. He checked my parents' papers, indicated everything was in order, stamped their visas and said, smiling, they could go to America. It was like hearing a prison sentence commuted. I handed him my papers, including the military exemption. He looked a bit surprised when he saw it. He studied the exemption, said, "However," then paused. -However- To this day, when I hear the word, I break out in a cold sweat. The consul didn't have to say another thing, I knew I wasn't going to the United States. He informed me my name had not been included in the affidavits my brothers had sent from America and that I had to write asking them to add it. Until that was accomplished, the consul couldn't grant me a visa.

Herman jumped out of his chair shouting, "How come you didn't tell us that three months ago when we could have done something about it? Now it's too late!" Once war had started in September, postal communication between Slovakia and the west was interrupted. The consul politely said he was very sorry but nothing else could be done at that time. The fact was that something else definitely could have been done. Had he wanted to, the consul could have waived the omission of my name from the affidavits as an inconsequential technicality and issued me a visa then and there. Whatever the reason, he chose not to. As we left his office, I had my first real sensation of hopelessness. It would not be my last.

A few weeks later we cheered with mixed emotions as my parents left for America. We were, at once, happily relieved to see them on their way to sanctuary and dreadfully apprehensive about what lay ahead for us. We found out soon enough.

A new restriction affecting the company became law. A Jew was now forbidden to have controlling interest in his business. Instead of the forty-nine/fifty-one percent arrangement, the Aryanator was given fifty-one percent and the Jew no more than forty-nine percent, and often less. Final say in all business matters now rested with the new owner, regardless of his expertise, or lack thereof. Despite the additional loss of revenue, we still considered ourselves lucky to be dealing with Jan Malik. Fortunately for Herman and me, it was business as usual. For many other Jewish ex-proprietors, the law had its intended strangulating effect.

With the economic phase of the restrictions well underway, the next step was to confine the Jews. Consistent with its policy of Judenrein, the government decreed that we could no longer live on the main streets of Slovak cities. Businesses were unaffected because they were already Gentile-owned. Jews had thirty days to relocate. Anyone not meeting the deadline, for any reason, was evicted, forfeiting all possessions. The authorities didn't care where we moved, as long as it was off the main thoroughfares. The main street in Presov, formerly named Masarykova before the Republic's partition, was now called Hlinkova. (After the war, it was renamed Stalinova.) Herman lived at Hlinkova 67.

Buildings along Hlinkova Street were typically European. They were two or three stories high, attached, and ran the width of the block. Each building had large doors at the front and rear, wide enough to accommodate a horse and buggy. The wider door was inset with a smaller door for pedestrians. Inside the front entrance was a courtyard leading to a stairway that went to the second floor. The landlords's apartment was at the front of the building, facing Hlinkova Street. Our office was toward the rear. A half-flight up from the office were four other apartments that ran to the rear of the building facing the back street, Jarkova Street. Herman's apartment was the third one back.

For some reason, the restriction's wording actually said that no Jew could live in a residence where the windows *faced* the main street. Jews living on Hlinkova Street in middle and rear apartments were not required to move. On a technicality, our landlord, a Jew, had to vacate and Herman and his family were spared dislocation, for the time being. The technicality notwithstanding, a month after the edict was posted, the press proudly proclaimed Hlinkova Street to be Judenrein.

With confinement of the Jews underway, trips to the kiosk every few weeks were charged with increasingly greater trepidation. Each new posting cost us another freedom. We were being systematically impounded from society, forbidden to: attend public school; hold public office; go to public functions-concerts, theaters, movies; be in public places-parks, swimming pools, spas; have radios; have telephones (except for business); be on the street between seven p.m. and seven a.m. For any breach of those laws, we were subject to immediate arrest. Worse, with arrest you became known to the authorities. In the thousands of discussions Jews had every day about how best to weather the storm and avoid trouble, the guiding wisdom was: be invisible.

We tried to make the best of things, thankful we still had the apartment, the family together, the business intact-though no longer ours-and the society of our close friends. But the psychological effects of our gradually worsening situation were consequential. It was unpleasant to be in public. I felt undesirable and unwanted. Wherever I went I'd go out of my way not to be conspicuous. In buses and trains, although the law did not yet require it, I went to the rear of the car. Discrimination was the psychosis of the times. I shunned association with everyone except family, close friends, and the lumberjacks.

The Germans needed plenty of lumber for the war. The mills in Slovakia operated at capacity. I worked almost every day, doing either paperwork in the office or supervising the lumberjacks in the forest. Finding it difficult to concentrate in the office, I preferred the distracting rigors and long days in the woods. The lumberjacks were outgoing, free-spirited, and scornful of the campaign against the Jews. They were fun to be with and never protested being supervised by a Jew.

The dilemma of the time was that, privately, a substantial number of Gentiles, including clergy, were unhappy about the treatment of the Jews. Publicly, it was another matter. People were afraid to speak out. Intimidation prevailed. There may have been a chance for public disapproval had the Pope made a strong statement against the policy toward the Jews. But without such a declaration from the shepherd, what could anyone expect from the flock?

Catholicism in Slovakia was a more influential force than politics. So much so, that it was a paradox of the war that as Slovakia's Jews were going to the slaughterhouses in Poland, Slovak synagogues remained open for the dwindling number of Jews left. It was against Catholic doctrine to deprive anyone's religious freedom. Slovak authorities were not about to challenge the Church.

When I worked in the woods, I looked forward to the lunch break. As I ate my sandwich, the lumberjacks grilled their bacon, caught the drippings on black bread and told dirty jokes. I laughed, salivating at the same time, not from the jokes but from the bacon's aroma. As I eyed the succulent black bread, the lumberjacks passed it under my nose urging me to take a bite. "God won't punish you," they heckled. "It's a treat and you deserve it with what you're going through. Besides we're in the middle of nowhere, who'll know?"

"He might," I replied, the uncertainty of God's retribution still a deterrent. They laughed, slapped me on the back, and devoured their lunch with a gusto that made it all the more tempting. Eventually, I did succumb and ate the bacon. As much for its irresistible smell as for the further opportunity it gave me to enjoy the lumberjacks' camaraderie. The bacon was delicious but after the first few bites, I stopped on reflex and waited. Nothing happened. The relief on my face was obvious and they roared, "Hey, you're still alive. He didn't strike you down. Have more bacon."

I told them of an incident when I was going to school in Presov and living with Herman. I was twelve years old. Alice had a friend who suffered from tuberculosis. A superstition held that ham was a partial cure for TB. When her friend visited weekly, Alice, who wasn't religious, sent me to the store for ham for her friend. It unnerved me each time I went but I had to do what I was told. The store sold only pork products. The dense aromas were so savory that with each visit the temptation to taste the ham grew stronger. One day, carrying the ham home, I opened the package and ate a slice. My first reaction was disappointment. It didn't taste as good as it had smelled. My second reaction was dread, I was going to get sick and die. I grew up having it drummed into my head that if I ate anything from swine, that's what would happen as punishment for not observing the dietary laws. Was I going to get it from God! When I got home I went right to my room and started praying. For hours I asked God to forgive me. I said the evening prayers with special emotion, promising never to touch traif again if He would forgive me and let me live. I kissed the mezuzah fastened to the molding of my bedroom door dozens of times. Herman came home and called me for dinner. I told him through the door that I wasn't feeling well and wanted to rest. I fell asleep emotionally exhausted, waiting for His wrath. I awoke next morning soaking wet but alive! Overjoyed and grateful, I thanked God profusely. For a long time afterward, I was a very good boy. The lumberjacks got such a kick out of the story, they howled and fed me more bacon.

So traumatic was the experience that it still confounds me how religion, canons and principles created for our well-being and salvation, as we were told growing up, can have devastating mental and physical effects on some and for others provide comfort and strength. It's an enigma how the faith that religious conviction engenders becomes either blessing or curse. Millions of Jews would be forced to deal with that enigma in the next five years.

To help relieve the stress the restrictions created, our clique got together on Sunday afternoons. We took turns hosting our little soirees, duly chaperoned by one or both of the host's parents. We told jokes, listened to records, and did imitations of the day's popular singers. I danced with Maria, sneaking a hug or a kiss when the chaperons were distracted. The host's parents prepared the food and provided soda and liqueur. They took care to make a nice spread in the belief that not to do so reflected poorly on the family, including their child. The group had made a rule not to discuss our plight. Our get-togethers were strictly for fun. For those few wonderful, much needed, hours we pretended things were normal. Determined to enjoy ourselves, we created a make-believe world. As much as the camaraderie helped to buoy my spirits, it wasn't enough to keep them afloat under the Tiso regime's relentless propaganda barrage.

Day in and day out the press hammered the Jews: our sinister and profane ways; our debauchery and depravity; our defilement of decent societies not only today but throughout history, proving that we are mankind's lepers; our being the cause of the war that Germany was now justly and gallantly pursuing against us. I felt demoralized and dehumanized.

Discrimination works! Being put down so often eventually keeps you down. Humiliation becomes ingrained. Even today when I see a Jewish person in the spotlight for having done something wrong, I feel uncomfortable and apprehensive that such prominence will provide anti-Semites with another opportunity to knock the Jews.

After each restriction, we didn't know what to expect next except that the new edict would be worse than the one before. We continued hoping for the best, unaware of the strategy behind the restrictions: to grind us down, isolate us, and take away our means of subsistence. In a phrase, to prime us for the "final solution." Each phase of the overall plan had stages.

The scheme to remove Jews from their businesses was in four stages. In one year, Jewish-owned businesses had become, first, forty-nine percent, then fifty-one percent, Aryan. In late summer 1940, authorities implemented the third stage. They ruled that large Jewish companies required three Aryanators to run things. Malik and Company had to accept two more Hlinka party members as "partners." This time we did not have a say in choosing them, they were appointed.

We had the luck to draw rational opportunists. Stefan Ripka, an assistant bank manager, would help Jan Malik "run" things in Presov and Andrej Andrejko, who lived in Svidnik where we had our saw mill, would assist in "administering" operations there. They knew nothing about the lumber business but were discerning enough to see that we did. They had the good sense to keep hands off. They claimed to be Party members only because it made their lives easier, affording them such benefits as revenue from Malik and Company, for example. They had nothing personal against Jews, they were simply living with the times. They collected their checks each month and left us alone.

The steps taken against the Jews, purging them from

economic life, humiliating them, and depriving them of rights were vested in law. Slovakia's President, Father Dr. Tiso, justified his government's policy toward the Jews in speech after speech.

> We are criticized for taking radio receivers away from Jews. Well, what of it! There are more important things than radio receivers. People come to us with complaints that we are taking away their shops, their enterprises, and contend that our actions do not behoove the Christian religion. And I say to you that it is very Christian. For we are taking what the Jews took from our people. Their leader Moses commanded the Jews that on the Jubilee Year all property shall revert to its original owner; but the Jews appear to have forgotten this law! According to the Talmud a Jew who cheats a gentile is doing the will of God, and therefore it is a religious commandment to cheat him. Know, my brothers, we are only taking what is rightfully ours. Our policy is based on the Christian principle of brotherly love.

Times were tough though not yet life-threatening. We missed being part of Presov's hustle and bustle; we missed the good will of our fellow citizens; we missed luxuries we once took for granted; we missed acceptance and security; and, most trying of all, we missed peace of mind. Still, a Jew had a place to live, food to eat, clothes to wear, parties to attend, temples to pray in, and a God to hear those prayers. And there were signs of hope. Though France had been beaten, England was fighting on and winning the Battle of Britain. America was now helping. Things seemed to be improving. They weren't, of course, as we were about to find out. Near the end of 1940 military activity in Presov escalated dramatically.

For the second time since mid-1939, when they had massed troops for the invasion of Poland, the German

Army was back in force. After Poland's surrender, the Germans had been discreet about showing their presence in Slovakia, wanting the people to think President Tiso's puppet government was independent of Berlin. The only way to spot the few German officials around was by the Nazi party pin in their lapels.

Now movement of German soldiers and materiel was at pre-invasion levels. Day in and day out vehicles rumbled through the city heading north and east. When troops stopped for the night, homes in Presov-Gentile, of course-were appropriated to billet the soldiers. This went on until the end of June 1941 when Germany invaded Russia.

With so many Germans around, Jews tried to be more inconspicuous than usual. We weren't always successful. Most Slovak Jews spoke both Slovak and German, most Slovak Gentiles spoke only Slovak. German soldiers needing help to converse with a civilian sometimes asked a passing Jew to interpret. Walking to the office one day, a soldier stopped me to do a translation. I shook in my boots standing at attention before him, trying to be as efficient as I could and get away as fast as possible. Before dismissing me, the soldier said with a half smile in a seeming attempt to be friendly, "You're Jewish. Not very good. Not very good." He walked away shaking his head. The formidable German presence in Presov had a chilling effect. It created a palpable feeling of entrapment.

On top of this, two new restrictions constituted the first serious threats to our survival. One restriction was the fourth stage in the plan to take all businesses away from Jews. It ordered that ownership in a company had to be one hundred percent Aryan. The new boss was free to hire the former Jewish owner as an employee, but the Jew could not earn more than the previously directed one thousand crowns per month. The new owner could fire the Jew any time he wished, without notice. For a while, most Jews were kept on the job to teach the business to the new owner.

Herman and I were able to continue operating our lumber company as usual, except for one significant change: our incomes had been decimated. We took home one thousand crowns a month apiece-one hundred forty dollars total, less than half our usual income.

Our depression plummeted to a new depth. Our rights had been seriously violated. We had no means of appeal and no one was trying to help us. We saw things only getting worse. They were. The other restriction was rationing.

Rationing affected everyone, Jews and Gentiles. As usual, it hit Jews harder. For some warped reason, everyone was allotted the same number of ration stamps. But Jews, still reeling from twenty months of one restriction after another, had a harder time coping. To make sure the equity in the allotment of ration stamps didn't give Jews a chance to recover their equilibrium, yet another restriction became law.

Twice a week, on Monday and Friday, people did the bulk of their shopping for meat, fowl, dairy products, and produce at the Farmer's Market. Now Jews were permitted to shop only after eleven in the morning. With food already scarce because of the war, most items were gone by that time which, of course, was the government's strategy. Our struggle to survive had escalated. Finally, it dawned on us: we were in real trouble.

Chapter 4

Schemes

Our main concern had been to protect ourselves. Rationing turned concern into obsession. Schemes for self-preservation abounded. Most promising were those enabling a Jew to hide his identity. It became an irony of the day that a Jew's surest way to "salvation" was conversion to Catholicism. Hundreds converted. They suffered no loss of faith, they just wanted to survive. With so many new conversions, authorities became suspicious. They ruled that only conversions made prior to 1939, before Slovakia became a state, would be considered valid. After that date, they claimed motivation to convert was highly suspect. Each case would be considered individually.

Another protection was to have a false baptismal certificate. One day my Aunt Miriam's son, Avram, came to the apartment with a plan to obtain one. He still sold lumber in Humenne and had the reputation for being a convincing salesman. Through a connection, he heard about a Greek Orthodox priest in a small village near the Polish border who issued valid baptismal certificates for five thousand crowns apiece-about three hundred fifty dollars. That was a lot of money even before the restrictions. His connection had explained that it was possible to obtain the documents because the Church in outlying villages was responsible for keeping vital statistics-births, baptisms, marriages, deaths-and the priests filled out the appropriate certificates by hand. I was uneasy about the idea because it meant conversion. That it was only on paper didn't make me feel any better. But when survival is at stake, you're desperate to grasp at any hope, any chance to save yourself.

I asked Herman if he wanted to get in on the scheme. He demurred, saying it would be more difficult for him to "convert" an entire family than it was for me to convert as a single person. Also, he was well known in the community and to the local authorities. Converting meant that he'd have to leave Presov. If he were caught, what would become of his family? Finally, he felt suspicious about the plan. It turned out he was smarter than I.

The day of the trip, Avram and four of his friends from Presov picked me up in a taxi rented from one of his acquaintances. The six of us were in high spirits the entire four-hour trip. The prospect of getting the baptismal certificate and, as a result, relief from persecution was like adrenaline. The village was tiny so the parish house was easy to find. It was a plain, drab, building austerely furnished. The priest motioned us to sit down, then asked to see the money. We put thirty thousand crowns on the table. He nodded, said he'd be back shortly with the documents and left the room, leaving the money on the table.

Shortly, an officer from the border patrol came in. He spotted the money at once, demanding to know what was going on. Under the circumstances, any story we fabricated would make no sense, so we told the truth. He shouted that what we were doing was against the law. He raved about the gall of us dirty Jews defiling the Church in such a way. He threatened severe punishment once we arrived at district headquarters. We were under arrest! We sat there too petrified to move, let alone think about trying to make a run for it to the taxi. Then it dawned on me that the priest and the border guard were probably conspiring. The timing of the border guard's arrival with all the money on the table, just after the priest had left the room, was too coincidental.

I began to plead with the officer that he had nothing to gain by arresting us. We would give him the money if he just let us go. He stormed at me for trying to bribe an officer of the Slovak Border Patrol, threatening that we kikes were now in serious trouble and were really going to get it.

The priest came in not feigning very well his surprise at seeing the border guard. The guard explained that when he saw the taxi outside and us inside with all the money on the table he got suspicious.

I interrupted them to plead again, this time to the priest. I begged him to take the money and use it for his many good causes. Just, please, to let us go.

The priest and the border guard walked to a corner and started haggling, loud enough for us to overhear their badly played little drama. The priest asked that we be let go to show us Christ's mercy. The officer said we had broken the law and had to be punished, especially since we were dirty Jews. The priest replied that it wasn't Christ's way. The officer replied that he had his sworn duty to uphold. Finally, the priest told the guard to be a good Christian and let us go to set an example to the Jews. Apparently, that remark was meant to tip the "disagreement." They kept the money and released us.

The trip home was intense with mixed emotions. On one hand, we were severely depressed. By not obtaining the baptismal certificates, we were still vulnerable, to say nothing of losing all our money. On the other hand, we were immensely relieved not to be in jail or worse.

Despite the protection a baptismal certificate might have provided, that experience and thoughts of Father Hlinka, Monsignor Tiso, and those priests doing nothing for the Jews, soured me on turning to the Catholic clergy for any help. I thought about the remarkable priest in Dlhe wondering where his kind were.

Arranging to hide on a farm was another scheme many Jews tried to protect themselves. It was easier to conceal yourself in the country than it was in the city where the risk of being spotted by someone you knew was much greater. Being on a farm also gave you easier access to food. The difficulty was in finding a farmer willing to hide you and your family when the time came. If you found such a farmer, you paid him "insurance" in advance. There was no way of knowing whether he would fulfill the agreement or turn you in. Psychologically, at least, the agreement was better than having no agreement at all. Regardless of the money and despite the risk, many farmers wanted to help the Jews for humanitarian reasons.

Some Jews built bunkers in the woods. They were usually little more than holes in the ground, with straw inside to insulate against the damp soil. Leaves and dead branches were used to conceal them. The problems with the bunker were its impracticality in winter and the difficulty in storing food supplies.

In desperation, Jews tried anything to endure. Some placed hope in myths borne out of faith. They increased their prayer time, chanted special prayers, and became models of Judaism. Even my highly intelligent brother, Herman, succumbed to the entreaty of an ultra-Orthodox rabbi who lived in the neighborhood and sold remedy to the Jews' plight based on the Gematria, a type of number mysticism. The rabbi asserted that, in my brother's behalf, he could recite certain prescribed prayers and light a specific number of candles in a cemetery at a certain time on a particular day, thereby diverting the present threat to him and the Jewish people. As a religious Jew, Herman paid the rabbi to purchase the hundreds of candles required for the ritual. It was a way to give hope to those who needed something to hold onto and a way for the rabbi to eke out a living.

As reduced incomes limited access to markets and rationing took hold, bartering became widespread. Those selling critical commodities such as food stuffs, heavy clothing for winter, and lumber for firewood had an advantage. In the meat market, for example, if a ration stamp allowed you to purchase one pound of meat, the butcher could give you a bony piece or a fatty one. With something to barter, you would get one pound of all meat and, perhaps, a bit more. Our family's leverage was firewood. Our business also gave us the advantage of mobility; we had access to goods other Jews didn't. We tried to share as much as we could with less fortunate friends, but even with advantages the pressures on us just to get by were relentless.

Bartering became big business. Jews traded their furs, jewelry, and gold for food and other necessities. Never letting up, always looking for ways to deplete our resources, authorities passed a new regulation. Jews had to turn in all their furs to a government agency, newly created for the collection. Authorities claimed that it was a way for Jews to help the war effort. Soldiers needed warm clothing for the winter. Who knows what percentage of furs surrendered actually reached the soldiers and how many were sold for profit?

Then the government created the Gold Fund. It became everyone's patriotic duty to give what gold they had, so said the authorities. For Gentiles it was voluntary, for Jews it was mandatory. Slovakia needed the gold for international trade; the Slovak crown had little value outside the country. The gold was turned in to the banks, which gave receipts to the "donor," and then sold the gold to the government. Undoubtedly, much of the precious metal found its way into private stores. Jews tried to hide what gold they could but the law made it difficult and dangerous to do so. Jews caught bartering their horded valuables were arrested. In due time, the penalty would be deportation.

My sister-in-law Alice had always been overly protective of her family. The daily demand of having to devise ways to improve their lot had made her high strung and aggressive. One day, in an effort to refurbish her dwindling food supplies, she decided to go to the Farmer's Market before eleven. She put on a babushka and the full white skirt of a peasant woman. She wore no yellow star. Risking arrest on two counts, she went off to shop. Just as she finished shopping, a gendarme she knew stopped her. She had been caught. All she could do was make an appeal. Before she could think of a plea, he said, "Hey, what a cute peasant girl you make," then turned and walked away. As she related the story, shaking with relief, it reminded me of the gendarme who had let me go the day Herman and his family were arrested and of the border guard who had released us when we attempted to buy baptismal certificates. It was enervating to be always at some official's mercy, never knowing whether you would be pardoned or punished.

It was now 1941. Jews were faltering from the restrictions and more were in store. In late winter, a new regulation decreed that no Jew was permitted to live in a building that fronted a main street. With this law and the fact that a Hlinka party member wanted his apartment, Herman had thirty days to move from 67 Hlinkova Street.

Housing for Jews, already scarce, became almost non-existent. Two, three and, sometimes, four families were forced to share one small apartment. Jews who couldn't find a place in thirty days were evicted.

Herman found a small, three-room flat on a run-down side street a few miles from the office. It consisted of a living room, bedroom, and kitchen, a far cry from the apartment on Hlinkova Street. Luckily, he had to accommodate only his family of four. Sessi had moved into her own apartment several months before (eventually she went to Bratislava to be with her brother). I had moved from my cot in the office conference room into a one-room apartment two miles from Hlinkova Street with David Sekely as my roommate. Even though it was a tight squeeze for my brother's family, they considered themselves fortunate not to be sharing their living quarters with another family.

A few months after they moved in, a young Slovak Army officer named Kalinac, and his bride, rented the apartment adjoining my brother's. She was a peasant who knew little about being a housewife and less about the ways of the city. Alice befriended Pani (Frau) Kalinac by teaching her to cook, bake, shop, sew, do laundry, and outfit herself. Kalinac appreciated the attention Alice gave to his new wife and also became a friend. The relationship between the two families had to be private. It was dangerous enough for a civilian to consort with Jews, but for a Slovak Army officer and his wife to do so was career ending. At considerable risk, because informers were everywhere, Kalinac sometimes invited Herman, Alice, and I to listen to his radio. Jews weren't permitted to have radios and Gentiles who did were forbidden to tune to foreign radio stations, especially the BBC. We couldn't listen as a group lest we draw attention from a neighbor. As a precaution, Kalinac permitted us in the apartment only when he and his wife were not there. If we were discovered, they would be blameless.

The news wasn't good. It was fall 1941. Germany had swallowed most of Europe; North Africa belonged to Rommel's Afrika Corps; three German armies were sweeping across Russia, unstoppable. On the street, we began to hear rumors about Poland.

Presov was within 280 miles of all six killing centers in Poland: Chelmno, northwest of Lodz; Treblinka, northeast of Warsaw; Sobibor, northeast of Lublin, Majdenek and Belzec, south of Lublin; and Auschwitz, southeast of Krakow and only 125 miles from Presov. Though not all those sectors of Hell were up to speed by the end of 1941, it was inconceivable that it had taken almost two years for any news of what was happening to Polish Jews to trickle in. When it did, incredibly enough, it told little of what was actually happening.

We did not hear that Jews were being taken en masse, like cattle, to those centers and tortured, starved, worked to death, shot by the thousands in front of mass graves, and gassed in the backs of sealed vans. (The Nazis hadn't yet perfected their proclivity for dealing with human slaughter on a grand scale.) What we did hear was that Jews, uprooted from their homes, were in work camps. Germany needed laborers for its war effort. It wasn't good news, but it sounded reasonable and we believed it. Given the enormity of the crime being committed, who would have believed the truth? When irrefutable evidence supported the truth, most people, including the highest Allied officials, still didn't believe it. Even after the Russians overran Majdenek in July 1944, the first concentration camp to be liberated, the Western powers believed the reports to be more Russian propaganda than fact. The Germans took full advantage of the buffer human beings use against believing the worst. It was an ingenious strategy, whether deliberate or inadvertent.

In Slovakia, even after all we had been through, it was still beyond imagining where the restrictions were leading. We had no premonition that deportation was a possibility, despite the expulsion of hundreds of Jews to Hungary two years before. In early winter 1942 I sensed that, given the accumulating afflictions, it would be wise to flee Slovakia.

I approached my good friend Ludovit Argay with a scheme. He had not been doing well as a salesman so our company hired him part time. He also wanted to get out of Slovakia before he was drafted into the military. He not only strongly opposed the war but he was a staunch opponent of the campaign against the Jews. My scheme was to smuggle ourselves into Switzerland. He was dependable and trustworthy and I knew I could take him into my confidence.

The company had a contract to export charcoal to Switzerland. I planned to build a box, five feet by five feet by ten feet, and place it in the railroad car into which we loaded the charcoal. Charcoal was loaded loose. Once the car was filled with charcoal and hid the box, we would crawl into the box, cut a hole through the car's floor board for air, and be on our way. Ludovit, who knew mechanics, said he would build a motor with a belt leading from the hole in the floor to the wheel shaft under the train. As the wheels turned, the shaft would move the belt which would run the motor generating power to create heat. We'd be able to warm food during the trip, which we figured would take a week. I had no idea whether the contraption would work but Ludovit enthusiastically went about its construction. He said not to be concerned, that we were going to enjoy ourselves and have a good time.

Just days before we planned to leave, I read in the paper that the Germans had captured a group in Vienna trying to smuggle themselves into Switzerland in a freight train shipping charcoal. To conserve much needed gasoline, the Germans had invented a way to run automobiles on fuel generated from charcoal. Charcoal became a precious commodity and the Germans watched train shipments closely. We discovered that just in time. With conflicting emotions of crushing disappointment and considerable relief, Ludovit and I abandoned our plan.

In summer 1941, authorities devised still another scheme to extort money from the Jews. If a Jew dealt directly with Germans, he was eligible to apply for an exemption from wearing the yellow star. It cost twelve crowns to apply and another fifteen crowns for "administrative" charges when you received it. The exemption was valid for either thirty or sixty days after which time you re-paid the fees for a renewal. You could not renew before the exemption expired. Since the process took a few days, you had to wear the yellow star in the interim.

The government had determined it was demeaning enough for a German to have to deal with a Jew. Wearing the star in a German's presence was unnecessarily offensive. Herman and I conducted business with Germans on a regular basis. They didn't seem to mind the yellow star or us and we didn't mind them. Even if we did, we had no choice but to deal with them. It was either that or have no income.

I remember a buyer named Krosch. He worked for the German airplane industry, an interesting coincidence given my experiences four years later. When he entered the office to do business, he removed his Nazi party lapel pin so as not to offend us. When he left, he put it back on. He showed no outward sign of discomfort or revulsion dealing with Herman and me. In fact, one day I had to pick him up at his hotel in the company limousine. I waited in his room while he finished dressing. He was portly and his stomach hung over his pants. He kept struggling to tuck it in. He got one side under control, when the other side flopped out. This went on for some minutes. The more he struggled, the more annoyed he got and the funnier it became. I couldn't contain myself any longer and burst out laughing. Here was a Jew openly laughing at a German. Immediately, I became afraid but couldn't stop laughing. He, too, sensed the hilarity of the scene and also laughed. No doubt, had he been a different sort of German, that incident would have had more serious consequences.

Not wearing the star was liberating. I was still subject to all the restrictions but without the star I wasn't marked. I could chance going to public places. I wouldn't have to wait in back of a line for service. I wouldn't have to go to the rear of the bus. I wouldn't be stared at or shunned. I could imagine myself a first-class citizen once again. It was hazardous. If I were recognized, I could be arrested. Presov wasn't a big city, but it was large enough to chance it. After months of confinement, it was worth the risk. I was desperate to regain my self-respect. For the first time in three years I felt less oppressed, less burdened.

My heady feeling of relief lasted until the first day of spring 1942. At four a.m. on Saturday, March 21, deportation of Slovak Jews officially began.

Chapter 5

Spring Roundup

The alarm went off at seven. I got up quietly, padded to the window, and opened the curtains. The first day of spring was clear and crisp. The great valley beyond showed no sign of the greening soon to come, still it was tranquil and entrancing. Waters in the brook that bordered our sloping backyard, thirty yards away, were rushing toward the farmlands below. It was Saturday, which meant only a half day at the office. In the afternoon, I'd celebrate winter's official end with a walk in the countryside.

I let David sleep a while longer. He had a full workday ahead as an employee in the photography store he once owned. I also didn't want to confront him just yet. I was miffed from the night before when he pulled a fast one on me.

After work at six o'clock, we usually met in front of the Cafe Berger, a coffee house close to where we worked, walk the few miles home, and enjoy an evening snack. We ate our main meal at noon, he at his parents' apartment and I at my sister-in-law's.

I arrived at six and waited twenty minutes. No David. I wasn't wearing the yellow star, it was cold, so I went into the Cafe, had a cup of coffee, and read the paper. It got dark, seven o'clock came, still no David. I said the hell with it and went home.

I reached the apartment about quarter to eight. The key was turned in the lock. I couldn't get in but I could see through the key hole. David was dozing in bed with Sophia, the secretary from his brother's office supply store. Angry as I was, I let them be. I walked around outside in the cold for three-quarters of an hour. When I returned, the door was unlocked, Sophia was gone and David was sleeping blissfully. Given my temper, it was just as well.

Waiting for David in the Cafe, I considered what could have delayed him, not without concern. A tryst with a girl in our apartment wasn't a remote consideration. It just was not done. Good girls, and Sophia was considered a good girl, didn't go to a man's apartment. There were whorehouses for that sort of thing. Once I calmed down, I was probably more surprised than angry about the entire event, and maybe a little jealous.

When I woke David for work, I decided not to mention his thoughtlessness or the girl. I felt it was his place to apologize. Getting ready for work and during breakfast of a roll and coffee, we talked of this and that but he didn't broach the subject of the night before. On our walk into town, we said little, becoming distracted by an unusual amount of activity. People were rushing about, distress clearly showing on their faces. Obviously, something had happened.

David never did bring up the previous evening and I'm glad I hadn't made an issue of it. A week later, he would be gone.

We stopped to see David's brother, a clerk in the office supply store he used to own. Maybe he knew what was going on. Very upset, he told us that at four that morning gendarmes had gone to the home of the younger sister of a family friend and issued her a summons to report to the city's largest Hebrew school by nine a.m.

She was to take no more than twenty kilos of belongings. Apparently, the same scene had been repeated throughout Presov and surrounding districts in the household of every unmarried Jewish girl sixteen and older. The action came as a complete surprise to everyone, Jew and Gentile alike.

David, his brother, and I tried to come up with answers to the obvious questions. Why single girls? Why the notices at four in the morning? Where were the girls going? How long would they be gone? Why was this happening now? Then it hit me: Maria!

Spontaneously, I became another of the anxious Jews dashing about. It took me five minutes to run the half mile to Maria's apartment, a few blocks from our office. When I pulled up, out of breath, she was sitting on her rucksack in the walkway crying. Maria's mother was standing with her arm around her, also in tears. Her step-father saw me from the window and ran out waving the summons.

Its look and language were official. According to paragraph such and such, in government decree so and so, you hereby are ordered to report to Free Hebrew school by 9:00 a.m., 21 March 1942. You are permitted to take no more than twenty kilos of belongings. A list of punishments followed for not reporting, including arrest and deportation. The document cited nothing about the purpose of the summons, where the person was going, or for how long.

Instinctively, I told Maria to come with me. Her mother wanted to know where I was taking her. I said I just wanted to talk with Maria for a while in private. We'd be right back. Her step-father protested that he and his wife would both get into trouble if she wasn't at the Hebrew school by nine.

I took Maria to my office and put her in the small conference room that had once served as my sleeping quarters so she wouldn't be seen. I told her I had something to do, that I'd be back in an hour or so. I warned her to be quiet and not to leave the room. On the way out, I told the secretary, whom I could trust, that no one was to go into the conference room.

It's remarkable how the mind works in a crisis, indeed, that it works at all. In the short time it took to rush Maria from her building to the office, I thought of a way to try to save her. The summons looked like a conscription order. I reasoned, what else would they be doing with single girls but sending them to work for the war effort?

Military law allowed anyone called up for duty in wartime, who wanted to marry before going to serve, an exemption from waiting the customary thirty days. Usually, once a couple applied for a marriage license, notification of the pending marriage had to be posted publicly for one month before a license was approved. That gave sufficient time in case someone had a legal or personal objection to the marriage. For a person called to duty, the posting period was cut to one week, sometimes less.

Another law, established during wartime, mandated that any Jew considered by the government to hold an economy-important job was eligible for a work exemption, thereby releasing him from conscription. The work exemption also protected the Jew's wife, children, parents, and in-laws. Herman and I were deemed economy-important Jews and already held work exemptions. By marrying Maria, she, her mother, and step-father would be protected from conscription.

To accomplish my plan, I'd have to act with great dispatch. The marriage license had to be secured that day or Maria would be taken. Government offices closed at noon.

I rushed to City Hall and took the steps, two at a time, into a room lined with dazed Jews who had thought of the same scheme. The difference between us was that they were wearing the yellow star and I was not. It was the saving difference. As the guard was occupied trying to keep the queue orderly, I walked past them into the clerk's office.

Herman and I were well known around City Hall. Company activities often required us to obtain official documents of one kind or another. The clerk was friendly, we exchanged cordialities, then he asked me what I needed. I told him straight out that my girlfriend received a summons and I wanted to marry her. He was aware of the roundup and commiserated with my plight, but said he could do nothing. I needed a special dispensation that only the Zupan could authorize. The Zupan's office was in the Zupanate, a half-mile away. I rushed out, passing the still long line of cheerless souls.

Running to the Zupan's office, I began to feel the pressure. It was already nine thirty. The guard curtly asked my business. He said I had to see the secretary first. After a ten minute wait, the secretary told me the Zupan would not be in that day, I had to see the Assistant Zupan. I said fine if he had the authority to attend to my problem. She assured me that he did but he wasn't in at the moment. She expected him back in half-an-hour.

The Assistant Zupan was a well-known lush. Undoubtedly, he was at the corner tavern drinking. To seek him out might do more harm than good. I couldn't chance it given what was at stake. I ran back to our office to check on Maria and tell her what I was up to.

Meanwhile, since it was already well after nine and she hadn't reported to the Hebrew school, gendarmes had gone to Maria's apartment looking for her. This I discovered on my way back to the Assistant Zupan's office when I ran into Maria's step-father on the street heading toward my office. He demanded to know where Maria was. I told him she was in a safe place, not to worry. He said the gendarmes had come looking for her threatening that if she didn't report to the Hebrew school in one hour, they would take him. He was angry and afraid. I tried to mollify him by saying it was just a threat. They were taking only young girls. They wouldn't know what to do with an old geezer like him. He didn't appreciate the needling but I appreciated less his being more concerned about protecting himself than about protecting Maria. I reassured him that the gendarmes would not find Maria and certainly were not going to take him.

I returned to the Assistant Zupan's office at ten fifteen. He was in, half loaded, expansive, and glad to greet a fellow forester. He had worked in the Forestry Service before his current appointment and still took pride in wearing the Service's green uniform with its gold leaf epaulets. Among his official duties was to oversee the lumber companies and their contracts with landowners.

We reminisced a while but I was in no frame of mind for small talk. I blurted out my problem. Like that, he said, "Okay," in a tone that conveyed "done." He instructed me to go into the Registration Room down the hall, fill out the application for the dispensation, then bring him the completed forms. I wrote so fast my script was barely legible. Twenty minutes later, I had the forms on his desk for approval. He said it would take him half-an-hour to process them. I should come back at eleven fifteen. The dispensation would be ready then.

Again, I returned to our office to share the good news with Maria. She was tense, fearful of the bureaucracy. She imagined all sorts of obstacles from meddlesome officials and their interminable paperwork.

As I left the office on my way back to the Assistant

Zupan, I encountered two gendarmes in the hallway. They asked me where Malik and Company was. I pointed the way then quickly got out of the building. I had a hunch they were looking for me. The secretary told me later that indeed they were. One gendarme had even remarked that he bet the guy they had seen in the hallway was the one they were after. It was a close call.

I reached the Assistant Zupan's office at eleven fifteen sharp. He was busy with another appointment. I had to wait. Each tick of the large wall clock seemed prolonged, as if the second hand were stuck and moved only on some unseen, mechanical urging. When it finally ticked the second away, the sound seemed thunderous. At precisely the time the big hand centered itself between the V and the I, the Assistant Zupan called me into his office and handed me the dispensation to my unimaginable relief. He reminded me not to forget the one thousand crown fee payable to the Gold Fund. Besides the decree passed the year before requiring Jews to turn over their gold and jewelry to the Gold Fund, many government permits and licenses also required a "contribution" to the Fund to become valid. Once I paid the fee, I had to bring proof of payment, with the dispensation, to the marriage license bureau at Town Hall. I gratefully thanked the Assistant Zupan. He shook my hand, wished me good luck and with a smirk, added, "You'll need it."

A thousand crowns-about seventy dollars-was a great deal of money in good times. With the restrictions, it was a fortune. I had only part of the money. The fee was paid at the bank which closed at noon. It was eleven forty.

I raced to my brother's apartment to ask Alice what she could spare. Always the practical person, she kept a few extra crowns hidden for emergencies. We scraped the money together. It was now five to twelve. Breathless and soaked through with sweat, I reached the bank just as the guard was hanging the "Closed" sign on the large, ornate, glass door.

I motioned vigorously for him to let me in. He shook his head pointing to his watch and the sign. I waved the thousand crowns shouting, "For the Gold Fund." Good patriot that he was, he opened the door. The bank clerk and I quickly transacted the business. He stamped the document PAID. I had done it!

It had been a hectic and decisive morning. Instinct had impelled me to take chances I would not have taken had I been more rational. Crisis teaches you about yourself. But I wasn't out of the woods, yet. All would be for naught without the actual marriage license.

Back I rushed to City Hall. Luckily, the clerk I had first seen, what seemed like many hours before, was still there. I gave him the dispensation and the stamped Gold Fund receipt. He stared at it in disbelief commenting that it was the only one he had seen that day. He said his office was officially closed and to come back Monday for the marriage license. I pleaded with him, explaining that if I couldn't marry that day, my girl friend would remain vulnerable for conscription, adding, that the gendarmes probably were looking for her as we spoke. I apologized for being so persistent, trying to impress upon the clerk that it was just about a matter of life and death. He looked at his watch. "It's twelve thirty," he said, "have your bride and two witnesses back here in fifteen minutes." I couldn't believe my luck. I leapt out of the chair assuring him, as I rushed out the door, that I'd return in fourteen minutes.

Running at full speed to our office, only minutes away, I racked my brain trying to think whom I could commandeer as witnesses. The office closed at noon, probably no one would be there. Mother luck was still with me. Herman and a close family friend, Ernst Martin, were taking care of some last minute business. Out of breath and stumbling over my words, I quickly brought them up to the urgent second and the problem at hand. I grabbed Maria and the four of us ran back to the clerk's office with seconds to spare. The marriage ceremony took only a few minutes; it was perfunctory. But in those precious few minutes, Maria became my wife and, hence, ineligible for conscription, as did her mother and step-father. After congratulations, the clerk reminded us that the law also required performance of a religious ceremony to make the marriage legal. I assured him we'd take care of that the following week.

I had been very, very fortunate. Of all the Jews desperately seeking the precious dispensation that day, I learned only one other had been successful. Exemption from wearing the yellow star had given me advantage; knowing the right people had given me privilege.

As Maria and I were being married at City Hall, the first group of single, Jewish girls collected at the Hebrew school were marched to the train station and loaded into box cars. In all, three hundred and fifty were taken that day in Presov. By mid-afternoon they were on their way to who knew where?

A month later I found out. I received a postcard from Alice Roth, a girl I used to see on and off before Maria and I became involved. She was taken in the roundup. The card was postmarked, "Oswiecim." At the time, beyond the fact that it was a town in Poland, the word didn't mean a thing. Neither did its German name, Auschwitz. She was writing to say that she and the other girls were fine. They were working in factories and being well treated. I sent her a package of dried bread, dried fruit, and cookies. I didn't hear from her again.

Of course, the card was a lie. The Nazis' coverup

of their "solution" to the "Jewish problem" was a carefully orchestrated, ingeniously executed, deception. Undoubtedly, three factors contributed to its success. Two, were the intent and scale of the crime, which were literally beyond belief. The third, was the understandable human reaction which held to the hope that the purpose of the transports were what the authorities had claimed.

Alice Roth arrived at Auschwitz as the camp was getting up to speed and prisoners were needed to help with camp administration. Once the administrative hierarchy was in place, camp officials, apparently, were loathe to exterminate trained help. Training new help would take precious time from the killing. A relatively high percentage of women from that first transport held on to life until liberation. As I discovered several years after the war, Alice Roth was one of those fortunate few.

The week before our wedding Chupah, Maria stayed with the Martins as a precaution, though the transport of single girls had been completed and the search for her discontinued. The surprise roundup had made us apprehensive. Who knew what the authorities would do next?

Much of the community, including the Gentiles, was in tumult, shaken by a government that sanctioned the taking of young girls from their homes without warning, even Jewish girls, and transporting them with no indication where they were going or for how long. The public conceded it was about time the Jews were made to do their part for the war; they were Slovaks, after all. But not that way. To wrench people from their homes so inhumanely showed a citizen's vulnerability to the impulse of authoritarian policy. To the Jews it confirmed, at long last, just how committed the Tiso regime was to expunging them from Slovak life. And still, the dark purpose of the conscription wasn't so much as a remote musing. It was our common assumption that unjust and disruptive as the roundup was, those called up were working in factories in Poland. They were not in life-threatening danger. The postcards so many Jews had received from the girls attested to it.

The public outcry against the summary conscription of single Jewish women in no way inhibited the master race's master plan. The following Saturday, March 28, the day before the Chupah for Maria and me, they took all single, Jewish men, sixteen years and older. Their summons ordered no reporting time. Too many girls had eluded the dragnet the week before. The men were handed their notices, then taken straightaway. The women had been treated tactfully. The men were harassed and pummeled.

After the women were taken, David had premonitions. He felt he'd be safer staying with his parents. If the authorities decided to take single men, they'd look for him at our apartment not at his parents' home. In fact, gendarmes did come to our apartment for David. I learned later an informer told them where he was. When they came for him at his parents' home, he jumped out of the window and fled. Gendarmes and Hlinka Guard were everywhere. He was easy quarry: a young man running through the streets with a yellow star sewn to his jacket. David was caught and never came back.

It was a simple, sedate, marriage ceremony. The call up of David and the other single men created a pall over the affair. Who could celebrate? Only Herman, Alice, Maria's mother and step-father, the Martins, in whose apartment the affair was held, and a few other close friends were invited including a longtime friend of Maria's family, Dr. Ilona Myer, a well-known, highly respected obstetrician. We invited just the minimum number of males to satisfy the religious requirements of the Chupah and only the few others to avoid calling undue attention to the ceremony. The roundups had created a gnawing uncertainty about what the authorities would do next. Obscurity creates a sense of invisibility, a false sense, as events proved.

Ours was a marriage of expedience. Maria and I cared for each other but we weren't in love. I was reminded that until recent history, more marriages than not were expedient: to ally nations; to join powerful families; to carry on a legacy; to acquire property; to gain a dowry; to attain social standing. This marriage secured protection from conscription for Maria, her mother, and step-father. Had my parents still lived in Slovakia, the marriage would have protected them, as well.

After the roundup of single Jewish men, the Judenrat strongly urged all remaining single men and women to marry as soon as possible. They repeatedly emphasized how one marriage could protect several people from conscription: the husband, the wife, both sets of parents, and the couple's siblings.

We had no honeymoon. We moved in with a family Maria knew, renting a bedroom and sharing the kitchen and bath. With housing restrictions so tight and unable to carry the expense of an apartment alone, I had no other choice.

Once the turmoil generated by the roundup of the single men subsided, things returned to what had become "normal." We went about our daily routines in constant states of tension and apprehension. From the moment we awoke in the early morning, until we fell into our troubled sleep at night, the same questions ground at us: what was coming next and when? We knew further persecution was inevitable. Still, we had no idea of its ultimate consequence.

A week after the wedding, my sister-in-law came to the apartment and burst into our bedroom distraught. She wasn't crazy about Maria so she had no compunction about interrupting our privacy. Though Alice understood the circumstance of our marriage, she felt I should have done better. It was a typical mother's, or in this case surrogate mother's, reaction that no woman was good enough for her "son."

Alice's sister had called from Zilina, frantic. Her son George, an only child, had been taken. He was in a holding camp set up just outside town. She had tried everything to contact him but couldn't get anywhere. My sister-in-law demanded I leave for Zilina at once to see what I could do. We were a close-knit family, always there for one another. Understandably, she was upset. Also, I had a travel permit so I didn't consider it untoward of her to insist that I make the trip.

Zilina is about 110 miles northwest of Presov, close to the Polish border, a grueling seven hour train ride. When I arrived, I assured Alice's sister that I would do everything I could to locate her son. It had no affect on her despair. I went to the holding camp but couldn't get near it. Roadblocks were in place and Hlinka Guard were everywhere.

Despite my inability to get near the camp, I learned that George was already gone. Both the Judenrat and the Slovak authorities kept records. The Judenrat's register, kept for the Jewish community, recorded who went to the work camps. The Slovak ledger was tallied for the Germans who paid the Tiso regime on a per-head basis.

The record keeping notwithstanding, it was impossible to find out where George was sent. The Judenrat didn't know. The Slovak authorities didn't know. When a transport left Zilina, engineers were changed along the way. No one could be exactly sure of its destination, other than it was headed for a work camp somewhere in Poland. The explanation seemed logical, therefore it was easy to accept.

I returned to Presov with the news about George. The family was upset, of course, but hopeful that he was in a camp with decent working conditions. We comforted ourselves with the expectation that it was just a matter of time before we'd hear from him. A few weeks later, they took Alice's sister. George was never heard from again. Nor was Alice's sister.

In early April, a lull followed the first official recall of single Jewish women and men. There was no increased harassment, no unexpected government action, no roundups. There was also no relief from the incessant tension that had every Jew guessing what would happen next. It was all we thought about. It was all we talked about. The lull only heightened anxiety. Anticipation became worse than event. But life, such as it was, went on.

Company business remained brisk, the Germans needed ever increasing amounts of lumber for the war. I continued working at the office and in the woods. Moving about gave me some relief from my interminable trepidation. Maria stayed home most of the time, going out only when necessary. Socially, life was limited to family and a few close friends. Making new friends was dangerous.

After the public outcry at the taking of the single Jewish women and men, the government had explained that each citizen had to do his share helping in the war effort. Jews could not serve in the Army, therefore, it was only fair to conscript them for work duty. The government also justified taking unmarried persons as humane because they had no family responsibilities, hence, disruption to family life was minimal. The government reminded citizens that single Jewish men and women were exempt from recall if they were in ill health and had a doctor's excuse, or if the individual was the family's breadwinner. Few Jews obtained exemptions for either reason. Most Slovaks accepted the government's explanations. They made sense and many thought they reflected well on their leaders' decency.

The actual reason that single women and then single men were taken in separate roundups was due to the limitations of the killing centers in Poland. They were not entirely ready to handle large numbers of Jews in March and April. By May 1942, they were.

Early that month, two ominous signs alerted to a new action being imminent. One, was the increased number of Hlinka Guard in Presov, their forbidding presence made all the more obvious by the almost daily marches in their black, SS-style, uniforms. The other, even more foreboding sign, was the rescinding of the law that exempted breadwinners without work exemptions and their families from conscription. That left only economy-important Jews, their wives and children, protected from a call up. In other words, my exemption no longer protected Maria's mother and stepfather; almost every Jew was now fair game.

The government explained its new policy by claiming that more manpower was needed for the war effort. Rather than call up part of a family, thus breaking it up, it was more compassionate to recall the entire family, thereby keeping it together. That way a family could go about its life at the work site in much the same way as it had at home. That new ruling expedited the first mass deportation of the war.

The mad rush to government offices for work exemptions was on. Profiteering flourished. Hundreds of phony work exemptions were issued. In the end, they didn't help. Authorities caught most of those who held them.

Although Herman and I had legitimate work exemptions, I became fearful that one day authorities might question our company's need for two exemptions and, being the junior "partner," take away mine. Given that apprehension, the Hlinka Guard's increased presence and the rescinded law, premonition got the best of me. I decided to leave town. If there were a fire, it was best to be away from the flames. Once you were picked up, regardless of your circumstance, exemption or not, that was it. There was no appeal, no escape. And if they took me, they would certainly take Maria.

It was May 10, a Sunday. The company had a contract to harvest trees at an estate near Kysak. How bittersweet was the memory of Kysak and the beautiful Hungarian aristocrat who gave me my first lesson in the artifice of women. I was to be there Monday to start work, but I sensed I'd be better off if I left as soon as I could. The problem was that I needed an official reason to travel. Jews were forbidden to be on the streets Sunday. Maria couldn't come with me, women simply didn't accompany men on business trips. Even if social conventions permitted it, she didn't hold a work exemption, therefore, she had no way to obtain a travel permit. She was safe enough staying out of the way in the apartment.

The estate's executor was Jan Raslavsky, who also happened to be an assistant district supervisor. My strategy was to ask him to accompany me to the estate that day, introduce me to the owner, and show me around, none of which was necessary for me to do the job. I went to see him that morning. I leveled with him about the tension in the air and my sense that something dreadful was about to happen. He agreed to make the trip.

We took a carriage to the train station although it

was only a mile from his office. It was too risky walking the streets with Hlinka Guard out in such force, even accompanied by a government official.

At the estate, Raslavsky introduced me to the owner Gnadige (Honorable) Frau Kesselbauer. He explained that I would be supervising the timber operation and whatever assistance she provided would be appreciated. Half an hour later, Raslavsky took his leave and returned to Presov.

Frau Kesselbauer was in her seventies. She had been the mistress of a Hungarian aristocrat who had left her the small castle in which she lived and a thousand acres of land once used for his hunts. She had social standing but, except for the property, little wealth. She lived alone with a butler. Much of her income came from timber. She grew fruits and vegetables on her farmland and sold what she couldn't use for extra income. Hunters provided her with meat and fowl.

Monday evening her brother came to dinner. She invited me to join them in a delicacy of the aristocracy: quail. I had never eaten quail before and after that night I never wanted to eat it again. They prepared it by first letting it sit for about a week, until the insides decayed. Then it was cooked. When it was carved at the table, I almost passed out from the stench. Out of courtesy, I forced a few pieces into my mouth, praying I could keep them down. It was like eating excrement. Subsequent visits to Frau Kesselbauer's estate were always accompanied by the considerable uneasiness that I might again have to endure the aristocracy's idea of a delicacy.

Early Tuesday morning, Frau Kesselbauer sent her butler to Presov to find out what, if anything, was happening. Sure enough a mass roundup of Jews had begun late Sunday afternoon. This time the gendarmes had taken entire families, collecting them at one of Presov's largest synagogues. Once the temple was packed, gendarmes locked the hapless people inside until nightfall when, under cover of darkness, they marched the Jews to the train station and loaded them into transports. Then another group of Jews was collected, packed into the temple, and marched to the transports. This went on until daybreak Tuesday. When the transports pulled out that morning, five thousand of Presov's seven thousand Jews were on their way to "work camps" in Poland.

Their homes were sealed off. Officials, major and minor, appropriated what they could. There was no accounting. It was another bonus for being a loyal party member. Whatever was left was later auctioned with proceeds going to the government.

The May deportation created another public uproar. Even some clergy joined in the protest. Government response reiterated the Jews' obligation to serve their country and the humane way authorities were allowing them do it. Questions raised about appropriating Jewish property were countered by claims that Jews had been parasites long enough; it was time they gave back what they had stolen and hoarded. In the end, people sighed, threw up their hands and rationalized: the war would be over someday and the Jews would come home.

I returned to Presov from Frau Kesselbauer's Tuesday evening. Even had I not known, it was apparent something profound had happened. The Jews who had been spared winced as they walked, as if they still heard the hopeless cries of their brethren being herded away, struggling with their worldly possessions-crammed into two suitcases-as they were shoved into box cars. Three-fourths of Presov's Jews had been uprooted. Men, women, married, unmarried, rich, poor, healthy, sick, children, infants, were gone. Every remaining Jew had a story about a family member or friend called up. Theories abounded about why so many Jews were taken: the war was going badly; the populace resented the Jews not being called upon to do their fair share; they finally needed the Jews to bail out the Tiso regime. Worse, or perhaps better, no one had a clue about what their brethren encountered once the trains pulled through the gates of the "work centers" displaying the maxim, *Arbeit Macht Frei* (*Work Makes You Free*).

It was the same old cycle. Each new government action was a shock, worse than the last. We tried explaining away its intent, deluding ourselves with the hope that things would get better because they couldn't get much worse. We recovered as well as we could and persevered. With the cooperation of the Slovak government, the Nazi deception was working, superbly.

Paradoxical as it was, Slovak synagogues remained open for prayer. And pray we did, though many attended services with considerable cynicism. Prevailing wisdom had it that this was no time to take the chance of getting into even more trouble with Him. Go to shul. We needed all His help that we could get.

With so many Jews called up, the dwindling congregations became vulnerable to hooligans from the Hlinka Guard. During services, the Judenrat posted guards near synagogues to give sufficient warning whenever a band of "patriots" was on the prowl. If they caught you, it meant a good beating.

Next to hunger, the emotional toll hit hardest. During the day, the gnawing uneasiness and unremitting tension were as corporeal as our empty stomachs.

We spent most of our free time consoling one another. The struggle to keep picking up the pieces grew harder. But we kept trying, always with the hope that loved ones and friends called up were in a decent camp in a decent job.

In June, there was another lull. What existence we

had gradually settled back into routine. We got up, went to work, had a meager main meal at noon, took a nap, returned to work, came home, tried to anticipate the next storm, and went to bed for another restless night. That month, Maria and I moved into her grandmother's large, ornate, house on the outskirts of the city. She had lived there with her daughter and son-in-law until they were taken in the May roundup. Maria's grandmother would have been shipped too had it not been for her colostomy. When the gendarmes went to take her, she showed them the bag. Colostomies not being then what they are now, they left her. With her grandmother alone, Maria had been going to the house almost daily to keep her company. She invited us to move in.

The house was in a development called Czatar Gardens, a city landmark, surrounded by beautiful, manicured grounds. It had two entrances, a private hanging bridge over the Torisa River which you crossed only if you had a key to its gate. Without a key, you had to walk a mile around the Gardens and enter through the public bridge. Because it was a large house, the Judenrat moved in two other families. Even so, compared to our one bedroom in the small, shared apartment, it was luxury.

Toward the end of June I had to travel to Margecany, a city about twenty miles west of Presov, to oversee a job our company was doing there. One day, I was working near a siding at one end of the railroad yard. We had brought a load of lumber from a nearby saw mill and were loading it into an open railroad car. It was a hot day. We took frequent breaks to cool down and quench our thirst.

From time to time I heard faint voices coming from box cars parked on the siding. Curiosity prompted me to walk toward the cars. When I saw the armed German soldiers, I quickly changed my mind. I returned to the railroad car and climbed back on.

Standing on the car, I suddenly heard a voice calling from the transport, "Uncle Joe, Uncle Joe, Uncle Joe." I looked in the direction of the voice. Framed in a small, barred window of a boxcar I saw my niece, Judy, Esther's daughter. I stood there stunned, unable to move, unable to think.

"Uncle Joe, Uncle Joe," she called again, "can you bring us some water?"

I called back that I would and ran to a yard supervisor. He was near the siding recording car numbers. I pleaded with him to let me bring a jug of water to my niece, pointing her out. He said no one was allowed to roam the sidings except train officials. He got the jug of water and went to one of the German guards with it. Pointing to my niece, he asked if he could give it to her. The guard shouted, "Nein, Nein!" He ordered the supervisor away from the train. I ran back to the car I'd been loading and climbed on top. Judy was still at the window grate.

Then I heard my sister Esther's voice call out from inside the car. I couldn't see her. She must have been holding up Judy. She shouted that Eli and Alfred were also with her.

I was frantic. Here was my beloved sister and her family in this terrible predicament, thirsty, packed like cattle in a steaming railroad car on their way to who knew what sort of work camp and I was helpless to do anything. The wonderful times Esther and I had growing up in Dlhe and in Spiska-Nova-Ves when I visited there after her marriage to Eli flashed through my mind. We had kept in touch by mail when the restrictions made it increasingly difficult to travel. I always liked Eli, he was a good husband and father. Judy and Alfred were bright, beautiful children. I always enjoyed playing with them. No doubt, my "on-the-job training" with Herman's children, Hedy and Paul, helped me to be comfortable with Judy and Alfred. My heart was breaking for them. I stood there. It was all I could do. I felt utterly desperate and feeble. Esther and her family were only yards away, but it might as well have been miles. I have never know such rending frustration.

Esther cried, "We have been travelling since last night. I don't know where we are going. I'll try to write. Kiss everyone for me."

They were the last words I ever heard my sister speak. Shortly, the train slowly pulled out. She and her family never came back.

Chapter 6

Messengers

The trip back to Presov was interminable. Anguish does that to time. The image of Judy's petite face framed in the narrow, barred, window of the box car, the sound of Esther's voice crying out from behind the bolted door, are forever burned into my soul. I begged God that they would be sent to an agreeable work camp and be strong enough to withstand the rigors that lay ahead of them. I tried wrenching consolation from the knowledge that their relocation was temporary and they'd be coming home after the war. I would miss them so until they returned.

Herman was heartsick when I told him. He made me swear not to say a thing to anyone for a while. I didn't realize it then, but he blamed himself for what had befallen Esther's family. He had promised to obtain a work exemption for Eli, claiming him as a Malik Company salesman. He already had succeeded in bribing an official in Bratislava to get an exemption for a local lumber broker. It tormented him that he hadn't tried harder to get the exemption for Eli first.

By mid-summer 1942, with most of Slovakia's Jews gone, deportations slowed. The stress on we who remained intensified. Out of Presov's seven thousand Jews, only one thousand were left, the so-called economy-important Jews. Odds of our being deported had increased six fold. Day and night we agonized over how much longer it would be before it was our turn and what we could do to protect ourselves that we hadn't done already. If a Jew lost his work exemption and hadn't arranged for a hiding place, the answer was: nothing.

Early in June, Maria's step-father was fired from his job in the shoe store he once owned making him and his wife eligible for call up. By law, when a Jew was let go the employer had to report it to authorities. Shortly after his dismissal, gendarmes picked up Maria's step-father and mother. Their conscription panicked Maria, who was already in a heightened state of anxiety. From the first mass deportation of single Jewish women in March, she hadn't felt safe, despite our marriage and my protective exemption. The shock of her parents' call up accelerated her motivation to go into hiding.

Jewish women were easier to hide than Jewish men. A woman could put on a babushka and a peasant dress and easily assimilate into her environment. No matter what measures a man took to conceal his identity, all authorities had to say was, "Unbutton your fly." Our Covenant with God gave us away every time. If it hadn't been for that Covenant, tens of thousands, perhaps millions, of Jews would have survived Hitler's gas chambers. I heard dozens of stories that attested to it. One involved four young Jewish men from Presov who went to Bratislava on business. Gendarmes stopped them, pushed them into an alley, and told them to unbutton their pants. For some reason, one boy hadn't been circumcised, the three others had. The three were arrested and never heard from again. The boy not branded by the Covenant was scolded for fraternizing with Jews and released. He survived the war.

Somewhere in our history, something went wrong. Why did God choose to seal the Covenant with Abraham by circumcision? Why did God decree that any male who does not undergo circumcision will be cut off from his people? There could have been a better way to bind the people of Israel to the Covenant. Clearly, His intent was not to harm the flock, but the result marked His people. It separated them from everyone else. Claiming to be His chosen people and carrying the physical manifestation of that specialness helped breed resentment against the Jews throughout history. The Covenant was a brand, like the scarlet letter. In the Hellenistic and Roman ages, when public nakedness was widely practiced, removing the foreskin was considered an abomination. As scapegoats, circumcision made Jews easy prey to find, resent, humiliate, abuse, segregate, exterminate. It made the scale of the Holocaust possible.

Since the first roundup of the single, Jewish girls in March, next to food and protection, our main concern was the welfare of loved ones and friends in the work camps. Herman and I tried every means at our disposal to find out about Esther, Maria's mother, her step-father and David Sekely. All anyone learned was that Presov's conscriptees were somewhere in Poland.

It wasn't until late summer 1942, five months after Slovakia's first mass deportation, when we began to receive first-hand news from work camps in Poland. Polish entrepreneurs had devised a scheme whereby they smuggled notes back and forth across the border between those in Polish work camps and their remaining relatives and friends in Slovakia. Unlike the death camps, work camps were accessible. Most were open settlements of barracks guarded by local authorities or regular army troops, not SS. The messengers surreptitiously circulated through a camp, collected the notes, sneaked across the border, distributed the notes, gathered return messages, with money enclosed, sneaked back across the border and made delivery. It was a profitable business, but dangerous.

If the Slovaks caught a messenger, it meant prison, if the Germans caught one, it meant death. The more trips a messenger made, the greater the chance of being captured. After three or four trips, he was on borrowed time.

In late August, Presov had its first visit from a messenger. He carried a packet of paper scraps scrawled with notes from Presov Jews in work camps around Lublin, two hundred miles to the north. He left the packet at the Judenrat office from where word of his presence was quietly circulated through the Jewish community. For his security, the messenger stayed out of sight when he was in town. Judenrat members delivered the notes to the appropriate homes with instructions that return letters, with money, were due at the Judenrat office within six hours. Half the money went to those in the work camps, the rest was the messenger's pay. What kept him from running away with the entire amount, at least for a few round trips, was the financial incentive to maintain communications between the work camps and the Slovak Jewish communities. Once a messenger decided it was time to end his "tour of duty" for safety sake, he absconded with all the money and a new messenger took his place.

Despite the gamble that our money would be stolen, it was worth the risk. At least a portion of it made its way into the camps and did some good. To do nothing was out of the question. It would have added to our already considerable guilt that most of our brethren had been deported while we were still lucky enough to be home. How lucky became apparent as we began to read and compare notes.

A note from Maria's mother said that she and Maria's step-father were settled and safe but miserable. He was working very hard crushing stone for a road. They weren't getting enough to eat. Living conditions were unsanitary and primitive. Their treatment was wretched.

She didn't think her husband could survive much longer. Many workers were dying from starvation and disease. She herself wasn't well. Could we please send money to buy food? It was our first hard evidence of life in the work camps.

All the notes carried pleas for money to buy food. It wasn't possible to send food packages. They were difficult for one person to transport, let alone smuggle, across the border. Even if smuggling food had been possible, there was precious little of it among the Jews to spare.

A few notes contained dark intimations that Jews elsewhere in Poland were much worse off than those in the work camps, enduring brutalities beyond imagining. There was mention of mass slaughter. Auschwitz began to mean more than the German name of a Polish town. Incredibly enough, many, including me, found the extremeness of those stories too fantastic to believe entirely. We attributed them to aroused imaginations of scared, homesick, overworked, underfed, souls living in deplorable conditions. I even took some complaints of Maria's mother with the proverbial grain of salt. She tended to be a "kvetch" and maybe she exaggerated somewhat to prod us into sending more money.

We were certain things were very bad and our breaking hearts went out to our fellow Jews. But mass slaughter? How insulating it is that the mind will not assimilate more reality than it can handle.

The messenger's visits were irregular. Sometimes he came each month, sometimes every two months. With each visit, it gradually began to sink in that, even if the stories coming from Poland were partly true, the matter was of the gravest concern. It also hadn't escaped our notice that postcards from the young men and women taken in the March roundup had stopped. Messengers hadn't heard a thing about where they were. For a short time, we had other sources.

In 1942, an underground network coordinated by the Judenrat was formed to smuggle Jews over the Slovak border, through Slovakia, then across the Hungarian frontier. Passing though Slovakia they were hidden in homes in the Jewish community. Traffic between Poland and Hungary was kept to a few families at a time, both to make the operation manageable and not to risk discovery.

Every now and then the Judenrat assigned a family to my house. It was large and relatively secluded. In the outskirts of the city it was a reasonably safe temporary sanctuary. One family, he was a wine merchant from Cracow, was the first to bring us news about what was happening to Polish Jews. The Germans had created ghettos to concentrate the Jewish population in the cities. Then they demolished the ghettos and moved its inhabitants to camps where conditions were beyond endurance. Jews were dying there by the thousands. Still, despite being closer to the German actions than anyone we had spoken with, and as horrendous as it was for the Polish Jews, the wine merchant had no inkling of the actual intent or scale of the slaughter.

The underground network was functioning with considerable success when, for some reason, the BBC made a broadcast ostensibly to praise the heroes who were helping Jews escape from Poland to Hungary. I never understood the motivation for such a broadcast. Naturally, it alerted the Germans and the network had to close down.

News from the work camps and from Polish Jews being smuggled through Slovakia into Hungary increased tensions another notch. With each new level of magnitude, you think you've reached the breaking point. Another escalation surely would be unendurable. But you discover that the will to survive is stronger than the temptation to give up. As life becomes more tenuous, it also becomes more precious.

On another front that summer, although we didn't know it at the time, a small committee of brave souls in Bratislava was attempting to bribe the German advisor to the Slovak government, Dieter von Wisliczeni, to halt deportations. He was Adolf Eichmann's right-hand man in Slovakia. The group felt it had nothing to lose and everything to gain by approaching Wisliczeni. Only a few thousand Jews were left in the entire country. It was a propitious time to test Wisliczeni's patriotism in relation to his greed.

Incredibly, not only did the bribe appeal to Wisliczeni, but he wanted to discuss it directly with Eichmann. If Eichmann approved, the deal was on. Arrangements called for fifty thousand dollars cash, not crowns, to be paid in two installments. After the first installment, deportations would stop. It was a vast sum of money for that time, especially in those circumstances. The committee had already collected twenty-five thousand which Wisliczeni received as the first installment in late summer. He halted deportations, declaring a six-week "truce" until he received the rest of the bribe. If he didn't get it, deportations would begin again. It wasn't lost on the committee that the six weeks ended three days before Yom Kippur.

The committee couldn't collect the entire second installment by the deadline. Two days after the truce expired, Wisliczeni ordered three thousand Jews deported. The roundup began Yom Kippur eve. Forty eight hours later, with the three thousand Jews inside the box cars, but still on Slovak soil, the committee finally raised the rest of the money and paid it to Wisliczeni. Exasperated by the delay, admonishing the committee that he was no one to be toyed with, Wisliczeni sent the transport to Poland anyway.

The few thousand Slovak Jews left in the country spent the next year in their ghetto homes still tense and fearful, most of them unaware of their comparative safety thanks to the bribe.

Winter 1942-43 was quiet, though no less anxious. Deportations had been suspended. News from Poland had ceased. Winter conditions made it difficult for messengers to cross the Polish-Slovak frontier, their tracks in the snow making them easy to pursue. War news did trickle through. Things had begun to go badly for the Germans.

Our newspapers and radio reported only propaganda, but they could stretch the truth just so far. We read between the lines and saw a pattern. The Nazis were consistently mounting "heroic" defenses that were always victorious. But each new victory was "won" nearer to Germany.

One day, I ran into a reporter friend. It wasn't advisable to be seen talking to a Jew in public so he gave me the usual, "Nice to see you, Joe. Would like to talk but I'm in a hurry." Then he added, with a wink, "I have to get to the office and file my story. Today, I'm sinking a hundred thousand tons of Allied shipping in the Atlantic."

The BBC authenticated what we suspected. We heard the Allies were running Rommel out of North Africa; the U-boats were being routed in the Atlantic; and the Wehrmacht had suffered a calamitous defeat at Stalingrad. Hopeful as these events were, the battlefield was still far away. We had to hold on. Fewer than a thousand Jews were left in Presov.

In May 1943, the first messenger of the year arrived from Poland. Winter had taken its toll. Maria's step-father had died, her mother and thousands of other Jews were starving. The plea to send money was desperate. The messenger stayed in town only one day during which time the Judenrat collected notes and money. The Judenrat delegated someone to secure the money overnight until it was turned over to the messenger. Whomever was nominated usually agreed, though it meant immediate arrest if he were caught. This time I was the "lucky" one chosen.

I brought the money home in a sealed envelope. Maria's grandmother advised that I hide it behind the grandfather clock standing in the foyer. That night I couldn't sleep for worrying about being caught. I don't know what prompted me but I got up, removed the envelope from the back of the grandfather clock and hid it under a floor board in the attic.

The next morning I went to work as usual. At ten o'clock, two officials from the Finance Office came to Malik and Company looking for Jozef Kornfeld. There was nowhere to run. With great apprehension I stepped forward. One official flashed his medallion pinned under his jacket lapel then ordered me to accompany them. I asked where and why. They motioned me to the door without response. In the car, I was told to direct them to my house.

In the continual stress and anxiety of day-to-day living, my stomach was never settled. As a result, it weakened my bowel. Only utmost concentration kept my insides from letting go on the ride to my house. It also took my mind off my fright. The officials rode in silence, for which I was grateful. I couldn't have concentrated and spoken at the same time. When we reached my home I pleaded to go to the shed house, running to it as I begged permission. One official followed me and stood guard outside. He watched me relieve myself. When I finished, he went in to check if I had thrown anything into the hole.

They searched the main house without a word. Maria's grandmother stood quiet and shaking. Maria was not home. The first place they looked was the grandfather clock in the foyer. After a short while of fruitless searching, they asked where the money was. Obviously, someone had informed on me. I had two alternatives. Either I could admit having the money, in which case it would be confiscated and I might avoid deportation for having confessed, or I could deny having it and hope they wouldn't find it. If they did, then I had no appeal. I'd be on the next train to Zilina. I decided to gamble. I replied, "What money?"

Without a word, they began searching again. It turned out that their action was a charade to extort money. Affecting frustration at not finding the money, they shoved me into the car and took me to the Finance Office. They put me in a room and left me.

I learned weeks later that Herman was in another office in the building at the same time trying to find out why I had been picked up. When he was told I was being detained, he spoke to the two officials who had arrested me. He tried to convince them how vital I was to Malik and Company; how much I was needed for an important timber operation that was about to begin; how important timber was to the war effort. They told him that if he paid twenty thousand crowns, they would release me. Herman shrugged his shoulders, "Who has that kind of money?"

I had fallen victim to another scheme the bureaucracy concocted to appropriate money from Jews. Authorities frequently arrested Jews rumored to have hidden money or precious jewelry. If the Jew couldn't pay the "fee" for his release, he was put in jail to think it over. If that didn't secure a payment, he and his family were in serious jeopardy of being deported.

While my brother was still in the building trying to bargain for my release, I was arrested and put on a train under guard. I wasn't allowed to see him or call the family. The train headed west. I was petrified that we were on the way to Zilina. I asked the guard our destination. He maintained a stern look and said nothing. I sat in silence and in dread, second-guessing why I had agreed to hold the money. Again, my fate was in someone else's hands and my destiny was about to take still another turn.

We disembarked at Liptovsky-SV-Mikulas, a city about seventy five miles from Presov. I was so relieved not to be going to Zilina that I was almost glad when I was taken to a small, grim, dirty-gray prison and thrown into an underground, windowless cell.

Another prisoner was already there. To my great relief, at least I wouldn't be alone. In a gesture of obvious respect, the jailer bowed slightly to my cell mate then slammed the heavy steel door behind me.

The man was sitting on his cot propped up by two downy pillows and covered with a heavy quilt. He was unshaven, slim, and looked to be in his late forties. Next to the cot was a table covered with delicacies. I couldn't believe it. I hadn't seen such plenty in a very long time: hard boiled eggs, cottage cheese, ham, kielbasa, and sitting in the middle of it all, a large chocolate cake. The food looked untouched. The spread so disconcerted me that before I had the presence of mind to introduce myself, I asked what kind of a jail this was? What was all the food doing here?

My astonishment amused the man. He presented himself as Dr. Por, a physician with some reputation as a gastronome; a nationally famous gastronome, so he claimed. To the Finance Office he was just another Jew with money to extort. In fact, he was famous. He had been in jail a week. When his friends and admirers learned of his arrest, they sent the delicacies which the guards were more than happy to smuggle to him. Not only for their "fair" share, but for the privilege of serving the celebrity in their midst. Government officials also knew of Dr. Por. He had been personal physician to the late Father Andrej Hlinka.

Once I got around to introducing myself, Dr. Por invited me to partake of as much food as I wished. He explained the great empathy he had for a person who loved music but had hearing loss; for the poor soul who loved painting but had impaired vision. He, too, had a passion he couldn't consummate. He was a gastronome with a stomach ulcer.

He told me that recently on a professional visit to a farmer, the farmer offered him a meal in payment. "I had to refuse it because of my ulcer. The farmer said that I may be the doctor but he had the cure for my ulcer. Out he brought a bottle of his homemade cherry brandy. I told him alcohol was the worst thing for an ulcer. He urged I try the cherry brandy anyway, insisting that I'd find it better medicine than any I had, despite what science said. I'm going to argue with a peasant? I took a sip of the brandy. To my surprise it was not only tasty but it made me feel good. I considered why the effect should be so salutary? I deduced that an ulcer is a sore. Sores need disinfectant. What is alcohol? A disinfectant. It made eminent sense. Who knows," he laughed, "someday alcohol may be the recommended treatment for stomach ulcers."

When we became better acquainted, I told him of my nervous stomach and the effect that continual fear and tension had on my bowels. He gave me his home address in Ruzomberok, a town twenty miles west of Liptovsky-SV-Mikulas. He invited me to come anytime for a physical exam. Obviously, he had no doubt his ransom would be paid.

He asked what had landed me in jail. As amiable as Dr. Por was, the past few years had taught me to trust no one. One never knew who was an informer. I was in jail because of an informer. By telling him, I would have admitted to my guilt. I blamed my arrest on the times and left it at that. That night, I felt my wariness may have been misguided. He offered me one of his fluffy pillows when we retired.

Except for the delightful Dr. Por, prison life was utterly uneventful. We were let out of our cell one hour a day to walk in a small circle in the narrow prison yard for exercise. The rest of the time we spent locked up. We were left alone-not bothered, not questioned, not harassed.

A week after my arrival Dr. Por was released for fifteen thousand crowns. He wished me luck and I promised to come see him if and when they released me. Alone in the cell the daily routine didn't change, except that I was now at the mercy of prison food. I also had more time than I cared for to worry about my fate.

A week after Dr. Por's release a guard opened my cell door, leaned in, and said I was free to go. I could pick up my train ticket and get directions to the station in the jail office. That was it. He walked away leaving the door ajar.

I looked like a bum. I hadn't bathed or shaved in two weeks. I didn't care. I was free! The trip home was long and wearisome. I was anxious to see my family, take a bath, and find out what had secured my release from jail. I was greeted like a returning hero. How wonderful it was to feel affection again, to hug and kiss and cry from joy. Alice put out goodies and we exchanged news about events of the previous few weeks.

Herman had negotiated my release in Presov for five thousand crowns. He told me it took two weeks of imploring to convince officials that he couldn't afford the original twenty thousand crown levy. They relented, agreeing to take fifteen thousand. It was another week before he wore them down to ten thousand crowns. They refused to budge another crown. He told me he said to them, "Then keep him." He laughed. He thought that was pretty funny. I failed to see the humor.

Only Herman could have gotten the officials to drop their price still lower. He was a superb businessman. He pointed out to the officials that the German government had been doing considerable business with the company he worked for, which was true, and that my not being there to help was causing delays in filling orders for the Third Reich. He added that by deporting me, the officials would receive no money at all. Five thousand crowns may not have been what they hoped for but it was better than nothing. They finally agreed.

I also learned that the day of my arrest, while I was being questioned at the Finance Office, Maria, despite her constant state of apprehension, had taken the money from the attic and turned it over to the Judenrat.

I was in jail two relatively quiescent weeks. Yet, the trauma of imprisonment had been psychologically maiming. Compared to losing my freedom, the restrictions and mental suffering of the previous five years were inconsequential. From that time on, whatever I did, wherever I went, I was vigilant about trying to anticipate where danger would come from next. I had to avoid arrest at any cost. I often wondered if anything could be worse than death. The war had taught me that captivity was worse than death. (Two years later, in the concentration camp, I would learn that there was something worse than even captivity.) No longer did I count on my work exemption or my status with Malik and Company as an economy-important Jew to protect me. In reality, I never could, of course. It just took me longer than most to realize it. Events during the summer of 1943 reinforced that conclusion.

Since fall 1942, deportations had almost stopped thanks to the gutsy bribe of Dieter von Wisliczeni. By summer 1943, Germany knew the war was lost. It became imperative to expedite the "final solution to the Jewish question." The Reich called upon its allies to increase shipments of Jews to Poland. The Slovak government was ordered to provide a transport of one thousand Jews every few weeks.

Jews who had lost their jobs and, therefore, their work exemptions, were picked up along with their families. Most of them were first shipped to the holding camp in Zilina. They were kept there until one thousand souls had been collected. Then they were taken to Poland.

Transports left Zilina on Saturdays. If a scheduled transport was short of the quota, word was sent to local police to pick up enough Jews from each community to make up the difference. The pickups were random. To ensure shipments had adequate time to reach Zilina by the weekend, Wednesday was designated, "roundup day." For us it became "crisis day." In those random roundups, it made no difference whether a Jew had a work exemption. The order was: grab them and ship them! The quota had to be met.

Although the inevitability of losing the war had spurred the Germans to fixate their attention on wiping out the Jews, many Slovak officials saw that being on the losing side meant judicial retribution after the war. The call for increased transports caught police between the survivors' future requital for carrying out orders and the Hlinka Party's immediate punishment for disobeying them.

Some officials resolved the problem, to an extent, by covertly letting the Judenrat know when a Wednesday roundup was imminent. After word was circulated among the Jews, it was up to each of us to find a hiding place for the day.

Given the importance of our company to the war effort, my exemption was more secure than most. But I was always mindful that our company had two exemptions and my brother's was the more important. I took no chances. In essence, most Jews were now fair game. When the Judenrat dispatched the Wednesday warning, I hid.

I got up at three in the morning, packed some food and, in the dark, walked into the nearby woods for a day of hiding. Maria went to the farm of a large family where she did part-time work as a seamstress repairing and making clothes.

I was lucky it was summer. It got light early and, except for rain, I didn't have to endure the elements. I passed the day reading-a book, magazines, the newspaper. I napped. I studied the trees and flowers. At four o'clock in the afternoon I crawled through a cornfield to where I could see our upstairs rear window. We had worked out a signal that if the gendarmes had come looking for me, Maria's grandmother was to put a towel in the window as warning. Throughout the day I prayed, "please God, let there be no towel showing." I thought about what I'd do if it were in the window, for that meant I was a fugitive and had to go on the run. The gendarmes usually completed their roundups by late morning or early afternoon. If the coast were clear by four o'clock, it was safe to come home. From week to week the impossible suspense ebbed and flowed. "Wednesday," became more than a day or a word, it defined the summer of 1943.

In July, Maria's grandmother died. Her death was the final upset to Maria's fragile insecurity. Ever since her parents had been taken, she felt increasingly vulnerable. She lost what little faith she had in the protection my exemption provided. Most Jewish women were more irritable and fearful than the men, anyway. Men had the distraction of their work. Women had to stay home with no relief from the monotony of their domestic duties, from trying to make ends meet, from worrying about when it would be their family's turn in the roundup. Maria decided to go into hiding. It was risky but she no longer believed she a had chance of surviving otherwise. She said that sooner or later, exemption or not, the ax would fall on us.

She had developed a friendship with a few families belonging to the Bahai faith. They farmed nearby and delivered our milk. They were unusually pleasant people and, consistent with one of their basic tenets: abolition of racial and religious prejudice, they were extremely sensitive to the Jews' plight. They also advocated equality of the sexes. They befriended Maria by giving her what produce they could spare and she, in turn, devoted what time she could doing seamstress work for them.

The Bahais gave Maria the name of a farmer who lived about one hundred fifty miles northwest of Presov, in a region called Spis, near the Polish border. A small concentration of German nationals lived there. She concealed herself as a peasant and became a farm worker.

We corresponded very little, once every month or two. To receive mail regularly in a rural area, especially with a postmark that was new to the mailman, would be suspicious and draw the authorities' unwelcome attention to the family with whom Maria was living.

No sooner had Maria departed than Herman received a phone call from Ernest Kovac. He ran our saw mill in Svidnik, fifty miles north of Presov. It had burned down. My brother and I were to come at once. The authorities were investigating the fire and suspected us of sabotage. In the climate of the time, being accused of anything was cause for alarm. But the main concern was how far the authorities would go to build a case against you. Innocence or guilt was irrelevant.

Gendarmes asked us where we were when the fire started? When were we in Svidnik last? What were our business relationships with the Slovak and German governments? What were our loyalties? Kovac, a German national, vouched for us and verified our responses. He also discovered the cause of the fire. It started in the engine room where the machinery was steam operated. A fire in the boiler was always going to produce the steam. Apparently a cinder had ignited the saw dust on the floor. After more questioning, to our thankful relief, the gendarmes released us.

The fire could have been a financial disaster but the company was diversified in both timber and charcoal production. Three months later the mill was rebuilt. Had it not been for the squeeze created by the reversal of German fortunes and the battlefield moving ever closer, we would have been back in full operation. It was a loss we didn't at all mind taking.

A few weeks after our return to Presov, Gnadige Frau Kesselbauer's butler came to the house with a note. She had to undergo surgery and asked if I would mind taking care of one of her dogs. I hadn't seen her for over a year, since we completed the timber operation on her property. During the project, we had developed a cordial relationship. It might have become a friendship had I been an aristocrat.

She had two dachshunds, Nula and her male puppy, cleverly named, Zero. Nula means zero in English. Nula had taken a liking to me. During visits, she would jump into my lap to be petted and to sleep. The note asked if I would take care of Nula for the month Frau Kesselbauer was in hospital to undergo surgery. She preferred to have her operation in Budapest, but would be unable to do so if she couldn't find a suitable home for Nula. Since Nula seemed to like me, would I do her this considerable favor?

Arrangements for Zero had been made. I told the butler that I would be pleased to take Nula and I was. I liked the dog. I also hadn't forgotten Frau Kesselbauer's saving kindness by allowing me to stay at her castle during the first mass roundup in May of '42.

A few weeks later the butler brought Nula and a letter detailing instructions for her care. I was to comb the dog every day, bathe her once a week, and feed her milk and bread once a day, making sure the milk and bread were fresh. When the dog had to go out she would scratch at the door three times. When she finished her business she would scratch the door once to come in. The letter also expressed her profound gratitude. She could face her operation with peace of mind in the knowledge that her Nula was being so well cared for. I had saved her life. The butler had also brought a small suitcase containing the dog's silver comb, silver eating tray, silver water bowl, fur coat, and woven sleeping basket with its cushion and hand-knitted cover.

The dog was extremely well trained, her comportment was extraordinary. If there were a canine equivalent to a princess, Nula was it. She had been with me about ten days, her daily routine never varying, when one day another dog appeared in the yard about lunch time. It barked once, Nula jumped onto the window seat, looked out, went to the door and scratched three times. She disappeared behind a bush to do her business, so I thought. The other dog had disappeared too. I paid no further attention. Half an hour later Nula scratched once on the door, I let her in and she jumped onto the window seat to look into the yard. The other dog was sitting on the lawn staring up at the window. Nula jumped down, went to her bed, and the other dog left. This went on for a week. Except for my impression of how intelligent and well behaved those dogs were, I thought nothing more of it.

Three weeks later the butler returned for Nula. He brought a warm note of thanks from Frau Kesselbauer for taking such good care of her Nula and the open invitation to visit her anytime.

A month passed. One day, I received a long letter from Gnadige Frau Kesselbauer. This one wasn't so warm. Did she clean me out! She wanted to know what kind of a degenerate I was. She thought she had been dealing with a gentleman. She should have known better than to trust a commoner. What I had done ruined her life. It ruined Nula's reputation. Could I imagine what Nula's puppy, Zero, now thinks of his mother? Had she known what would have happened to Nula she would not have had the operation. Under the circumstances, she would have been happy to risk worsening her condition. I was not welcome at her castle. She didn't want to know me anymore. In all that harangue she couldn't bring herself to use the word: pregnant.

I had no idea that the dog had gone into heat. What did I know about dogs? Although I was truly sorry I had caused Frau Kesselbauer such distress, I was flabbergasted by her lopsided sense of what was consequential. To carry on so about a dog in the midst of a time of indescribable human suffering was beyond me. She knew I was a Jew, that I was coping with bigger problems, like trying to survive. I never got around to responding to the letter. I did show it to friends. They got a grim chuckle out of it.

Toward the end of summer, Maria wrote that I should join her at the farm. Even with my exemption, she warned, I could never be sure I was safe. How long could I continue to live with such uncertainty? How long could I successfully hide in the woods?

There's no question I would have been safer at the farm. It was in a sparsely populated, out-of-the-way area where farms were a couple of miles apart. With all that had happened, irrational as it was, I felt better off in Presov. My decision was a consequence of both my self-deception that believed the lie about my security and the unwillingness to uproot my life.

On the farm I'd be in unfamiliar surroundings without the resources I had in Presov. I'd be doing work I didn't like, completely dependent on others and at their mercy. I'd be able to play the role of a Gentile peasant farmer only until a gendarme or, worse, a Hlinka Guard, asked me to open my fly. I'd be away from my family and the much needed emotional support they gave me. I wouldn't be there if they needed me. Then there was Maria. She was a good person, we had been friends for four years, but I didn't love her. I wasn't drawn to the prospect of living with her in such different and alien conditions. Maria asked me to come anyway. We could be together for a while and I could meet the people with whom she lived. What could it hurt?

The train station was ten miles from the farm. There were no cars or carriages. To my exasperation, after a train ride of four and a half hours, I faced a three-hour trek to the farm on foot. Obviously, Maria had started out very early that morning to be at the station for my mid-afternoon arrival, so I kept the displeasure of the unexpected hike to myself. On the way, we caught up on news and tried to make sense of the war.

It began to grow dark. We were walking through a wooded area. Maria began to glance around nervously. She was quite near-sighted so I thought her eyes were bothering her. She looked here and there, showing signs of panic. Finally, she sank to the ground. "I'm lost," she groaned, "we should have crossed a hill and been out of the woods by now. I don't know where we are." I may have been an old hand at spending time in the woods, but that was an enforced stay I appreciated not at all. We spent our night of reunion huddled against a tree, cold, hungry, and cuddling for warmth. Affection was the farthest thing from my mind, homicide was much closer.

We started out again at daybreak and, mercifully, she found where she had gone wrong. By late-morning we trudged up to the farm, starved, and bedraggled. The worried farmer and his family greeted us heartily. Their concern for our welfare boosted my spirits.

The two days I spent at the farm offset the emotional lift. It was a barren existence in the middle of nowhere. The farmhouse was small, with spartan furniture, what little there was. There were no books, no radio, nothing. To conserve kerosene and candles, there was little or no light once it got dark. The life was hard, isolated, empty. Despite the chance I took returning to Presov, I was glad to leave. I sensed the farmer was relieved, too. It was risky enough hiding a Jewess. Hiding a Jewish man was extremely dangerous. A curious neighbor passing by seeing a stranger working the farm could ask questions or, worse, report it to the authorities. If the stranger were a woman, all she had to do, if questioned, was be sure her story made sense. For a man, an official only had to say, "Pull down your pants," and the Jew, the farmer, and his family were finished.

I returned to Presov to continue my life and Maria stayed at the farm. Every few months, when her loneliness became more overwhelming than her fear, she made the long trip to Presov for a visit. She arrived in relative calm and left when the old apprehension began to set in.

Life went on, albeit, secluded, dull, and high-strung. For diversion, I played bridge with friends and talked. We talked about whom had been taken that week; how long the war would last; how much closer the Russians were; and ways we could avoid being caught between armies as the battlefield came closer.

By fall 1943, the years of constant tension and fear-the anguish of seeing family and friends deported, the trauma of arrest and imprisonment, the weekly threat of the roundup, the dash into the woods almost every Wednesday to hide, the close call with the saw mill fire-had gotten to me. Very little of what I ate, there wasn't much to begin with, agreed with me. I decided to take up Dr. Por on his invitation for a physical exam.

Ours was the reunion of compatriots who had suffered and survived injustice and ordeal. We told and retold our stories about life in prison. He asked how long I had stayed after his release, how much my brother had paid to get me out, and what I had been doing since?

Then he took me downstairs to his office for the exam. He stuck a tube down my throat into my stomach and pumped up acid samples every five minutes for half an hour. With each thrust he commiserated how unpleasant the procedure must be. As far as he could tell, I had no stomach problem. He suggested it could be my appendix. He recommended that I have it removed. His reason was not entirely medical. He explained that with conditions as they were, what with the always present threat of a roundup and the battle front getting closer, Jews would soon be forced to hide, most likely in the woods. If I should have an appendix attack under such circumstances, it could mean death. The organ wasn't essential anyway so I wouldn't miss it. Undoubtedly, it was good advice but I had a fear of going under the knife, so I put off the operation.

In late October, deportations slowed again. By winter 1943-44, they stopped. There were few Slovak Jews left to round up. Seventy thousand of the country's ninety thousand Jews were gone. In Presov, six hundred out of seven thousand were left.

At the end of March 1944, the Russians were at the

Slovakian border. They had reached Dukla Pass in the Carpathian mountains, only forty miles northeast of Presov. As they closed in, the authorities, including gendarmes and the fanatic Hlinka Guard, became shaky. With the end of the war in sight, they saw prison or a hangman's noose in their future. They grew friendlier toward the Jews. After years of constant tension, upset, and fear, we had a bit of relief. Not much but, combined with the hopeful news from the battlefield, the effect was euphoric. It was also short-lived. Another threat loomed: the danger of getting caught in the crossfire between converging armies.

Authorities ordered both Jews and Gentiles to evacuate likely battle areas. Jews had to be particularly wary. The German retreat west had increased their presence in Slovakia. It was one thing to be taken by Slovak authorities, it was altogether something else if the Germans got hold of you.

Alice grew more fearful. She had a remaining sister in Zilina and decided to move the family there. That way they would be a good distance from the battle zone which bought them time to wait out the German collapse. They left in late April. Herman oversaw the business from Zilina. Every so often, he made the trip to Presov to check on things first-hand. There wasn't much to oversee or to check; the lumber industry was almost at a standstill. I stayed in Presov to handle what little business we had. I didn't have a family at home anymore and I was the only one who could deal with our German- and Hungarian-speaking clients. But I did know that soon I'd have to leave Presov. It was time to obtain Aryan papers, otherwise my chances of surviving elsewhere were slim.

I turned to my oldest friend, Ludovit Argay. I needed a Gentile I could trust. One who would be willing to risk lending me his birth certificate and I.D. so that I could have an identical I.D. made, only showing my picture instead of Ludovit's. Ludovit assured me he'd help in any way he could.

Once I left Presov, I could use the Aryan papers because no one would know who I was; I could get away with being Ludovit Argay. If, for some reason, I was captured and they tried to check with the real Ludovit Argay, it was unlikely he'd be home. He was still a travelling salesman and on the road most of the time.

Soon after I had my new I.D., Ludovit came to the office with something from his mother. She sent a picture of the Virgin Mary for me to carry. Her counsel was that I should always keep it with me for protection and good luck. I put the picture in my wallet figuring that if I were supposed to be Gentile, then carrying a picture of the Virgin Mary was a good way to demonstrate it. I was touched by her gesture.

In mid-May, Ernest Kovac phoned me from Svidnik. He wanted to close the saw mill and take his family to Zvolen to live with his in-laws. Zvolen was about 100 miles west of Presov and just south of Banska Bystrica, a city that would soon be of considerable significance to thousands of Slovaks, including Herman, his family, and I. Kovac said the Russians were only twenty miles from the saw mill and partisan activity was increasing around Svidnik. As a German national he didn't want to fall into Russian hands. As soon as he said the word, "partisans," there was a sharp click. A voice broke in demanding to know, "Where are the partisans? Where is their headquarters?" Apparently, the Germans monitored long distance calls from anywhere near the front. I became so unnerved I hung up at once. I tried to remember if I had said anything incriminating. I told myself to make plans to get out while I could. It was advice well given but, unfortunately, not taken. Once I calmed down, I delayed action. There was a lull on the battlefield and deportations seemed to be over. When I did determine to leave, the decision was made for me and almost too late.

It was June 11th, a Sunday afternoon. I received a phone call at home. To this day I don't know who it was. The voice said, "Joe, get the hell out now! They're going to round up the rest of the Jews in the city today." Then he hung up. With the sharp click of disconnection something in me snapped. It was the most hopeless moment of my life.

Chapter 7

Fugitive

The warning struck like a concussion. I held the phone to my ear, I don't know for how long, paralyzed by fear. Gradually, the buzz of the dial tone penetrated my insensibility. "Please tell me what to do," I mumbled into the mouthpiece. I felt utterly helpless and alone. I paced the living room in a muddle talking to myself, swaying in despair, as if davening. "I have to do something," I said. "But what?" I replied. "I need somewhere to go," I pleaded. "But where?" I asked. "I need someone to help me," I declared. "But who?" I moaned. It was Sunday, legally I couldn't even go outside.

Never before or since have I ever felt such desperation and hopelessness. Not when I was in jail. Not when the Germans caught me. Not even in the camp. I feel the sheer terror of that moment to this day.

The instinct to survive eventually brought me around. I tried to collect my wits. I decided the hell with it, what's the difference between being trapped in the house or being caught in the street? At least if I tried getting away, I had a chance.

I put a few things into my briefcase-toothbrush, pajamas, and some business documents. If the gendarmes stopped me, my story would be that I was on official business. I'd tell them I had to be in Margecany early next morning. The company still had a timber operation there. They could verify it. If they asked why I was taking the afternoon train, I'd tell them that connections being what they were, leaving early was the only way I could be sure of getting there in time for the morning work. It was painful to think of Margecany. I still saw my niece, Judy, in that boxcar window pleading for water. I still heard my sister, Esther, crying out from behind the bolted door, "I'll try to write. Kiss everyone for me."

I locked the house. The other tenants, anticipating the roundup, had already gone into hiding. I started walking. I had no idea where. It didn't matter. I only knew that I had to get far away. The voice on the telephone carried life-or-death urgency. I understood how the fox felt when the hounds were let loose in relentless pursuit. If he made one error of judgment, it was over for him. But he never had a chance. It was hopeless for him from the start. He wasn't meant to escape.

The day was cloudless and warm. I hadn't walked far, yet I was perspiring, more from fear than from the heat. Few people were on the streets. Even for the Gentiles it was safer indoors. I took back streets. Every corner I turned I imagined gendarmes behind posts, hiding in alleyways, peering through door slits, ready to spring, like hounds, to corner me. In fact, few gendarmes were about. Most of them were mobilizing for the roundup.

Half out of my mind, my emotions let go. I began crying bitterly, wailing to God, "Dear God, what should I do? Where should I go? I've been a good boy. I've been religious. I've obeyed your Commandments. I'm in trouble! Please help me!" I trudged along, sobbing and talking to God, tears flowing down my cheeks.

I reached the train station. Approaching the ticket counter, I spotted two gendarmes sitting in the waiting room at the far end of the building. Slowly, I walked out of the station, trying to control my panic. I headed toward Solivar, a small village suburb four miles south of Presov, where Jan Hajduk lived. Our company had hired him as a log-loader, then promoted him to supervisor. I was instrumental in getting him the promotion. Though he lacked education, he was an able, dependable, congenial employee.

I arrived at his house by dusk, soaking wet, hungry, and utterly drained. As I dragged myself toward his front door, the neighborhood dogs announced my presence with vehement barking. Jan opened the door startled to see me. He saw at once that something was wrong. Hurriedly, I explained my plight. He quickly waved me into the house, glancing outside before closing the door. His neighbors were at their windows.

The house was small, consisting mainly of a large kitchen that also served as bedroom and living room. Off the kitchen was a small storage room. Jan lived with his wife, two small children, and his wife's father. They were asleep in the far corner of the room. He said I could stay the night.

He rigged a cot for me in the storage room. It was cramped but I was too grateful to care. Had the accommodations been luxurious it wouldn't have mattered. It was impossible to sleep. I couldn't stop my mind. It churned all night, the same thoughts besieging me. I knew I couldn't stay with Hajduk long. What would I do? Where would I go? I had little money. What would happen to me? "Dear God," I cried, trying to muffle the sound in my hands, "please help me!"

I began to comprehend what it was like to be a fugitive, hunted, with no place to go. Even today, a half-century later, I have empathy for anyone on the run, even a lawbreaker. When you're a fugitive you have no home. You're utterly dependent on others for food, for protection.

You scheme constantly how to evade your pursuers, second-guessing your decisions. You're in a constant state of anxiety, always on edge trying to anticipate potential danger at every turn. However you inflate the hope that somehow you'll make it, merciless fate usually finds a way to deflate it. I was terrified and lost. Despite the previous five years of sub-human status, I was not ready for the life of a fugitive; an animal on the run.

The next morning Jan came into the storage room. He was very sorry but he would be grateful if I could find another place to hide. His wife was extremely upset and afraid. Neighbors had seen me and someone might inform the authorities. I said I understood and I did, although understanding did nothing for my peace-of-mind. I asked if I could stay until afternoon. I needed time to figure out what to do. He nodded yes, we shook hands, and he left for his job at Malik and Company.

I sat in the storage room until late morning trying to decide what to do. My mind was "out of order." It was getting late, I had promised to leave and I did.

A few miles from Jan's house was a saw mill where we had transacted a good bit of business. I took a chance and went there to use the phone. It was a work day. People were in the streets so I didn't feel as exposed as I did the day before. I called the long time friend of Maria's family, Dr. Ilona Myer, who had attended our Chupah. She had good connections in high places. We had become close acquaintances working as part of the small group that coordinated the collection of notes and money to send to Poland via the messengers.

According to her sources, she learned that of the remaining six hundred Jews in Presov the gendarmes had found only a few dozen during the roundup (forty, to be exact). Apparently several authorities, in their continuing effort to make points with their eventual accusers, had spread word about the Sunday roundup throughout the Jewish community. Earlier the following morning-Monday-authorities declared an amnesty which, according to her sources, was authentic. Jews were free to come out of hiding without fear of being taken on the condition they relocate to western Slovakia. But, Dr. Myer warned, caution was definitely advisable. I almost fainted from relief. I felt as if I had a death sentence reprieved.

Officially, so said the authorities, the amnesty had been declared for humanitarian reasons, to get people away from a potential battle zone and allow the Reich's "heroic" army to prepare defenses in the area. Unofficially, that so many Jews had escaped the roundup embarrassed and outraged local Hlinka Party officials. They figured to catch them eventually. Strangers were usually self-conscious and awkward in an unfamiliar environment. The dislocated Jews would be conspicuous and easy prey when they moved west.

Dr. Myer's information proved accurate. Upon my return to Presov, I saw a few Jews on the street. Gendarmes were no more evident than usual. Businesses were open. It appeared as if nothing had changed. But my world had changed. I had changed. The day before I was a wary and fearful Jew trying to stay out of harm's way, concerned with keeping a business afloat, worried about his family, trying to wait it out until war's end. A day later, I had the mentality of the hunted. Never had I come so close to being caught like an animal in a trap. I had to get away. Amnesty or not, I felt the hounds in hot pursuit.

When I reached home, I threw myself on the bed utterly exhausted. The house was empty and deathly quiet. The other tenants had not returned and wouldn't. They stayed in hiding until the end of the war. I couldn't sleep. I lay there until the next morning.

At the office, no one said a word about the previous

day and I certainly wasn't about to bring up the subject. It was too draining just thinking about it. Business was slow. The spring rush of timber cutting and peeling was over. German orders were down along with their fortunes in the war. Herman called from Zilina urging me to let the business go and join him. I knew it was the smart thing to do, but an amnesty was in effect and I didn't want to leave home giving up the few creature comforts I still had, not just yet anyway.

In the few weeks after that awful Sunday of the "phone call," pressure on the Jews eased noticeably. The Third Reich was crumbling. Concerns of Slovak officials and Hlinka Guard were shifting from policy to accountability. Living with Herman and his family we'd be practically on top of each other. Food would be scarce. I'd feel like an interloper. The longer I held out in Presov, the better for them and for me.

As June wore into July, Presov swelled with refugees from the north fleeing the ever approaching battlefront. Most Slovaks were now being sucked into the vortex of war. They fled wherever they felt reasonably safe from the pillaging and destruction of the advancing Russians and retreating Germans.

By mid-July, business had come to a standstill, the Russian onslaught and lack of available railroad cars made it difficult to transport anything, lumber and Jews, included. The front had moved close enough to Presov for me to leave.

I packed only what I could carry and took the train to Zilina to join Herman and his family. They had moved into a five room apartment with two other families. Each family slept in a bedroom. The living room, kitchen, and bathroom were shared. I slept on the couch in the living room.

By August, the Germans were falling back rapidly.

As the fighting got closer, it became clear that Zilina would not be a haven for long. Soon we'd have to take to the woods to protect ourselves from the coming battle and the Germans. I decided it was time to take Dr. Por's advice and have my appendix out. No sense in taking the chance of an appendicitis attack while I was running for my life.

It was ironic in the madness of the time that, although a Jew was officially caste as less than human, subject to dozens of restrictions limiting his freedom and ability to survive, vulnerable at any moment to arrest and deportation, he was still permitted free medical treatment. Slovakia's policy of national health care entitled all its citizens to medical attention without cost. In the matter of national health, irrational as it was, Jews were still deemed citizens. As a company executive I qualified for no less than first-class care. Unlike the Germans, the Slovak government saw no policy conflict in permitting a doctor to treat a Jew.

Another paradox in that midsummer of 1944 was the relatively tranquil existence for the several hundred Jews who had migrated to Zilina, despite the ominous presence of the holding camp on the city's outskirts. We were far enough from the front not to feel endangered; few Germans were in the area and government pressure on Jews continued to ease. It was also for those reasons that the time seemed right to have the operation. I didn't feel at risk putting myself in the defenseless position of a patient.

After the surgery, the doctor told me he didn't understand why I had been advised to have my appendix taken out. Nothing was wrong with it. As I lay on the couch in considerable discomfort recuperating in my brother's apartment, it was news I could have done without.

It was the end of August. Forty five miles south of Zilina in the area around Banska Bystrica, a city of thirty thousand near the foothills of the Low Tatra Mountains, a Slovak uprising erupted against the Germans. Defectors from the Slovak army carried out the action abetted by a cadre of British and American officers.

Discontentment in the Slovak army had been building against the Germans for some time, even before the war started to go badly. From the outset, the German high command made it clear that they had little respect for the Slovak military. Slavs were an inferior people according to Nazi theory. Throughout the war, the Germans never permitted the Slovak army in the fight, even when they desperately needed its help. Its duties consisted mainly of servicing the German army's logistical needs. With the war all but lost, many Slovak soldiers felt it was time to ally with the winning side.

The uprising began with a crippling strategic blow to German transportation. Critical to an important east-west railroad connection was a tunnel in Vrutky, a main railroad supply line to the eastern front, fifteen miles southeast of Zilina and thirty miles from Banska Bystrica. By destroying it, the insurgents brought to a halt movement of men and materiel headed through that area toward the eastern front. Few German troops were stationed in the region to begin with. Potential reinforcements were busy with the Russians a few hundred miles away. The area was quickly liberated.

Word of the uprising spread rapidly. It elated most Slovaks, especially the few thousand surviving Jews. After six years of torment, dread, and despair, Jews were in reach of a Slovak oasis of relative safety. It was like being in sight of a promised land.

Herman decided to move the family there. He had a connection in Zvolen, sixty miles south of Zilina and fifteen miles from Banska Bystrica, the center of the uprising. Ernest Kovac, the manager of our saw mill in Svidnik, had fled to Zvolen with his wife and children. He was living there with his in-laws. Because I needed another week to recuperate from the operation, my brother planned our relocation for mid-September.

Meanwhile, a cousin from Bratislava, Max Ames, showed up. He, his wife, and son had been hiding there with Aryan papers for two years. When Max heard news of the uprising he made the long trip north to Zilina to learn more about it. He wanted first-hand information before deciding whether to move his family to the newly liberated area. According to our sources, the Slovak military was strong enough to hold the area until the Russians arrived. Max decided to return to Bratislava for his family and join us in Zvolen.

The few nights he spent in Zilina, Max slept in the living room on the floor. I was still on the living room couch and still in pain from the operation. It was difficult for me to move, let alone sleep for any length of time. With him in the room, sleep was impossible. Did he snore! Whatever I had within reach I threw at him-pillow, cane, ashtray, magazines, books, shoes. Each time I hit him he stopped snoring, turned over, then started up again, even louder. When he awoke the next morning he saw the debris scattered around him. He jumped up startled, wanting to know why we let him sleep through the air raid instead of taking him to the shelter. I told him there was no air raid but there should have been one. It would have been quieter. His snoring was worse than any air raid. Max wasn't amused.

In mid-September, we moved to Zvolen. The train was packed with civilians also fleeing to the newly liberated territory.

Kovac was very accommodating. He found us an

apartment, helped us to procure food and supplies, and assured us we could count on his continued assistance. We had excellent relations with Kovac when he was with our company. As a German national, though no Nazi, he was looking ahead to the end of the war no doubt to accrue all the good will he could.

In Zvolen, it was difficult to get our lives organized. It was a new environment. Except for Kovac and his family, everyone was a stranger. And we were at the mercy of the Slovak army's ability to hold the area until the Russians reached it.

About the middle of October rumors that the Germans were coming became epidemic. We had no illusion about our fate if we fell into their hands. Gentiles weren't much better off. There were grotesque stories of German atrocities against Slovak civilians, especially those suspected of being with the partisans or helping them. To set examples, the Germans had cut off ears, fingers, and hands, gouged out eyes, and cut out tongues. They hung people from hastily made gallows and left them dangling for days for all too see as a grisly warning not to cooperate with the partisans.

Two German divisions from the eastern front moved in to crush the uprising. For a few days, the Slovak army held out. Finally overwhelmed, they abandoned the fight, shed their uniforms, and eventually joined the civilians heading for cover in the woods. By the end of October it was over. That small oasis of freedom in central Slovakia became a wasteland. In March 1945, after the Germans were driven from the area, a mass grave uncovered near Banska Bystrica contained more than ten thousand slaughtered Slovaks.

Thousands-Jews and Gentiles-fled the Banska Bystrica and Zvolen areas in a mass exodus. They didn't know where they were running, just into the woods to hide from the Germans. Herman, his family, and I blindly followed the herd. Max Ames and his family, who had joined us in Zvolen, tried to make it back to Bratislava. The Germans caught him. No one ever heard from the "snorer man" again. From what I was able to piece together after the war, he was probably one of the ten thousand in that mass grave near Banska Bystrica. Somehow his wife and son got through and survived.

We fled into the countryside with no destination in mind, except to find a good hiding place in the woods. Two days and only fifteen miles later it was obvious that Herman couldn't keep his family on the run without being caught. Alice and the children couldn't endure the rigors of survival in the woods, especially with winter coming on. If they had to move quickly to avoid danger, it was unrealistic to expect women and children to keep pace with men.

We came to a small village in the middle of nowhere. I don't even think it had a name. Herman found a farmer willing to hide him and his family. The farmer agreed to dig out a large hole under the pig sty in which the four of them could stay during the day. There was no room for me. Had I imposed, it not only would have added to the discomfort of their "accommodations," it could have jeopardized the deal. The pig sty became their home for the rest of the war.

To be close to them I looked for a farm nearby to stay. I was able to remain there only a few days, until the farmer received word that the Germans were increasing their patrols in the area. I was forced to seek refuge in the woods on the outskirts of the village. Luckily, I stumbled across an abandoned army bunker. The Slovak army had built bunkers throughout the woods to help defend against German counterattacks during the uprising. Those defenses were no match in the face of two German divisions. Most bunkers were little more than well-camouflaged holes, ten feet by ten feet, with a small trap door to squeeze through. Fifteen people, mostly boys and young men, were packed into the bunker with hardly enough room for me. Shelters were difficult to find so I stayed.

The Germans picked up young Slovaks both to keep potential manpower away from the Russians and to ship them to work camps in Germany. The region had attracted thousands of young men due to its diminished military importance. Few German soldiers came to the area except to confiscate hay for their horses from the village.

The bunker was quiet. There was little conversation both to avoid attracting the attention of a chance German patrol and mutual suspicion. If you didn't know a person, you couldn't be sure whether he was an informer. Sometimes, even when you thought you knew a person, you couldn't be sure. I tried to be inconspicuous. As a Jew, I wanted no attention. We all may have had a common bond as refugees but anti-Semitism was too prevalent among Slovaks to expect the bond to be indiscriminate. My first night in the bunker I slept on the cold, damp ground, the only warmth came from the closely packed bodies.

I hid in the bunker during the day. At night it was relatively safe to emerge. Even under a full moon German patrols rarely ventured forth. They were easy targets for the partisans. I went to the village for food and to see my brother. It was always pitch dark due to the continuous blackout. Even the faint light coming through the grates of the wood-burning stoves was cloaked.

I established a routine. After I left the bunker at night, I washed and drank at a brook nearby. Then I went into the village to try to see Herman and buy food. Sometimes I arrived at the farm as he and his family were outside vigorously washing themselves. It was cold but not washing was worse than freezing. All day they lay in their hole under the pig sty trying to dodge the pigs' waste that dripped and dribbled through the cracks in the boards above them. It was a losing battle. The scene would have been amusing had the circumstances been less fateful.

Life for farmers in the region was hard in normal times, the war only added to their miserable existence. They were poor, isolated, lived in one-room huts, fed themselves from the land, and made little money. That went mostly to purchase kerosene, sugar, and salt. The sudden influx of refugees was a boon. Farmers sold eggs, chickens, potatoes, cabbage, carrots, and fruit to their new "neighbors" in the woods. Harvest had just ended so more produce than usual was available. Individually, though, the refugees had little money to spend. Diets may have been nourishing but they were skimpy.

By the end of that first week, most people had left the bunker. Some went further east, closer to the Russians, others felt it was better to be on the move instead of staying in one place, a few decided it was safe to return home. They acted on rumors: the Germans were moving into the area; the Germans were moving away from the area; the Germans were increasing their patrols; the Germans were decreasing their patrols; the Russians were getting closer, it was safe to come out of hiding; the Germans were throwing more troops into the battle, it was not safe to come out of hiding.

Only five of us remained in the bunker. I stayed to be close to my brother. Besides, where would I go? With more room in the bunker, I brought straw from the farm and made a crude mattress. I saw Herman, Alice, and the children once or twice a week. Sometimes I ate with them. Other times I brought a few potatoes back to the bunker to cook when it was too dangerous to stay out. It was important to conserve the little money I had, which was about two thousand crowns-roughly, one hundred forty dollars. There was no telling how long I'd have to hold out before the Russians came.

Three of those in the bunker were hiding to avoid being picked up by the Germans for work camps. The other man had been a member of the Slovak rebel army that rose up against the Germans. He was on the run to avoid capture and execution. His name was Mato Luptak. For some reason we hit it off.

I was wary of getting too close to any stranger for fear he would find out I was a Jew. I had kept my distance from the others in the bunker. With Mato, for some reason, I sensed no threat. I felt I could trust him, even though I discerned that, somehow, he knew I was Jewish. Then and in the months to come he never said a word about it.

During the day the five of us stayed in the bunker quietly telling stories and sleeping. One of the boys, Tom, had a small crystal radio with him. We spent part of the day trying to get more from it than crackling static. We never could.

At night, if I didn't visit Herman, my bunker-mates and I did favors for the partisans. They knew that of the hundreds of young men who fled the Banska Bystrica area, many were still hiding in the woods. They sought us out asking for our strong backs to carry boxes of supplies to their storehouses scattered throughout the sector. We were glad to do almost anything to help get rid of Germans, short of joining the partisans. We had heard what happened to captured partisans. I could imagine what they'd do to a Jew. Also, many partisan groups were anti-Semitic. Some groups eliminated Jews when they found them.

It was early November. From what the peasants in the village told us, it was only a matter of two or three weeks before the Russians would get there. The peasants hated the Germans for their pillaging and brutality. They were a big help to us.

I began to allow myself the luxury of believing that I'd survive the war. I was "comfortably" settled and feeling reasonably secure. How we are creatures of habit, able to adjust after only a short time to almost any situation, to almost any condition. As more refugees left the area, I reasoned that the Germans would decrease their patrols, perhaps even discontinue them.

Except for our few excursions with the partisans, the next several days were uneventful. Most people had fled the region. We heard the Germans had lost interest in the area except for their occasional forays into the village to confiscate food and hay. It was poor intelligence. Actually, the Germans had stepped up their daytime patrols in the woods because of escalating partisan activity.

It was about ten o'clock on a Sunday morning in mid-November. The five of us were relaxing in the bunker. It was quiet. A fresh snow had fallen, softening the stark, bare trees. Tom poked his head out of the trap door to take a quick look around. A German patrol was walking our way. Quickly he ducked from sight closing the trap door. He felt sure that they were too far away to have seen him. We sat stock-still, hardly breathing. As the minutes passed, I began to believe that Tom's intuition was correct, the Germans hadn't seen him.

Suddenly, a sharp, guttural, "Raus! Raus!" shattered the petrified stillness. Then, in German: "I will count to ten! If you're not out by then, we'll throw in grenades and blow you up!" The count began, "Eins, Zwei, Drei..." I told those closest to the trap door to open it and get out. Hands in the air, they slowly crawled out of the bunker.

It struck me that it was a Sunday. I had lived a

lifetime of Sundays. The Sunday of the spring roundup in March 1942. Two years later, the Sunday of the anonymous phone call in June. Now this Sunday when the Germans finally caught me. As I crawled through the trap door into the bright, white light, I thought, there will be no more Sundays.

Chapter 8

Capture

I was last out of the bunker. As I emerged from the trap door, a solider screamed, "Raus, Raus," jabbing the butt of his rifle into my back. I stumbled over to my companions, huddled together. When my eyes adjusted from the bunker's blackness to the snow-light of the clear, frigid, November morning, five German soldiers were standing in a semi-circle, their rifles aimed directly at us. A sixth soldier, their leader, was on top of the bunker above the trap door. He jerked his rifle upward. We raised our hands. He jerked his rifle sideward. We moved away from the bunker.

"Anyone else in there?" We shook our heads, too terrified to speak. He jumped aside, as he threw in a grenade. "If there was, he won't be coming out," he said, after the explosion.

Once the smoke cleared, he motioned another soldier to check the bunker. It didn't take him long. He crawled out of the trap door holding fragments of Tom's crystal radio. The damn crystal radio that never worked! Without so much as a glance at us, the patrol leader cranked a field telephone. He reported that he had caught five partisans in a bunker with a radio. He was confident we had been feeding information to the Russians about German troop movements. He was bringing us in for interrogation.

I spoke German so I understood what he said. I wanted to protest the mistake. I wanted to tell him that the radio was only a receiver; that it never transmitted anything but static; that we were hiding because we'd heard the Germans were taking young men and shipping them to work camps in Germany; that we had nothing to do with the partisans; that we were harmless. I couldn't. Few Slovaks spoke German, most Jews did. We were facing death, yet I had to stand there mute. If they realized I spoke German, I was doomed on the spot. Our only hope was to convince them we were innocent.

The patrol leader lined us up. Screaming "Los, los," he marched us off at gunpoint. Talking was forbidden. I was left to my thoughts. They were elementary: would I be hanged or shot? I became so weakened by fear I didn't know how far I could march. An hour later we came to a small command post at the edge of the woods. A few trenches had been dug. Several soldiers were milling about. It surprised me to see Hungarian troops with a Wehrmacht unit. The patrol leader repeated to a German officer the report he had given on the field phone.

The officer turned to us. He was casual and polite which made me feel a little better. He asked where the partisan headquarters was and how long we had been collecting information in the bunker. Once we told him we'd be free to go. Given his intonation, he could have been inquiring about the weather.

We tried explaining that we had nothing to do with the partisans. We were hiding from fear of being captured and taken to a work camp in Germany. Then what were we doing with a radio, he wanted to know? Tom told him it was his. It was only a receiver and never worked. The officer asked if we were partisans? Emphatically, we chorused, "no!" That was it. There were no more questions, no searches, no threats, no rough stuff. I began to hope he believed our story. He called for the patrol leader. I only overheard him say he had finished with us and to take us, I couldn't make out where.

As the patrol marched us through the woods, I tried to convince myself that we would be shipped to a work camp instead of being killed. We were better off to the Germans as laborers than as corpses. The longer we marched the more I let myself believe that's what might happen. We had been on the move about two hours when evening began to fall. We came to a small village, Lubietova, where the patrol decided to stay for the night. The partisans marauded after dark and the Germans wanted no part of that.

They put us in a school, locking us in a small classroom without furniture. Lying on the hard floor, trying to forget my hunger and apprehension, it hit me that I was carrying a thousand crown bill. If the Germans found it, they'd suspect me of being a Jew. The average civilian didn't carry that kind of money, especially in the middle of nowhere. And once they saw my covenant, they'd know I was a Jew. The I.D. I carried identifying me as Ludovit Argay, Gentile, wouldn't mean a thing. I had to get rid of the money.

I told the guard I had to go to the toilet, bad. He escorted me down the hall, waiting outside the door. There was no toilet paper so I used the bill to wipe myself. I pulled the chain on the flush tank above the toilet. The plumbing didn't work, either. Quickly, I pulled the bill out of the bowl and stuffed it behind the tank. When I opened the door, the guard ordered me to wait while he looked around the bathroom, then he dug through the mess in the bowl with his bayonet. Satisfied that I hadn't tried to get rid of anything, he prodded me back to the classroom.

Next morning we were given a slice of black bread and a cup of ersatz coffee. It was the first time we had eaten since our capture almost twenty-four hours before. It was meager but it gave me hope. Would they feed someone they intended to kill?

The patrol marched us about five miles to another village and into a small, grimy, squat building that served as field headquarters. Inside were soldiers wearing epaulets with the chilling twin lightning flashes of the SS. I sensed from the way my stomach began stirring, that I would not be able to hold whatever little was in it.

We were thrown into a tiny room containing only a bench. Two of my companions sat on the bench, three of us sat on the floor. We heard hammering behind the building. Through the small window we saw carpenters building scaffolding for gallows. No one spoke. Our plight was so hopeless there was nothing to say. I thought, "they're going to eliminate us then and there."

It was anguishing to think that no one would know how I died. I'd be leaving so many wonderful loved ones behind: Herman, who had been like a father; Alice, my second mother; their beautiful children; my cherished parents safely in America; Maria, my wife; my treasured friends from our clique. For what! I hadn't done anything wrong. I'd been a good person, a religious person, I had done what I was told, I worked hard, I harmed no one. I thought of all the good things that had happened in my life. Then I thought, maybe the gallows weren't for us. Maybe they'll shoot us. That would be better, I decided. With a firing squad I'd have a chance to survive. Their shots could miss, or hit me in the shoulder or leg. I'd play dead. Once they left, I'd run. Yes, I preferred shooting to hanging.

A strange calm came over me. A great weight lifted. I was no longer a fugitive. I was free from the constant terror of being on the run. I had done everything possible to survive. I had tried my best. It wasn't good enough. My time had come and I was ready. After the years of deprivation and fear, after months of being the fox in the hunt, death would be a liberation.

The door banged open. Tom was motioned out. I thought about the transition between life and death. Would I be aware of the passage? I tried to imagine what happens to the soul. How it left the body. I wondered if somehow I would sense its departure. The door banged open again, a soldier threw Tom into the room, his face bloody. Mato was motioned out.

I tried to imagine what it was like in the after-life. Where I'd be, what I'd do. Would everyone who had ever lived be there? Would I see the Patriarchs of the Bible I had so revered in my childhood? The door banged open. Mato staggered in. It was my turn.

I was taken into a room with two bare desks. Behind one desk sat an SS Untersturmfuhrer. An interpreter sat behind the other desk. The Untersturmfuhrer motioned me to step forward. He smiled and asked, almost cordially, where the partisan headquarters was located. I respectfully replied that I didn't know. "Then what were you doing with the radio," he asked. I thought, if it hadn't been for that worthless damn radio we probably wouldn't be in this mess. I told him the radio belonged to Tom. He had brought it into the bunker for some entertainment but it never worked. It was only a receiver. We had nothing to do with the partisans.

The Untersturmfuhrer said it was simple: if I didn't tell him where the partisan headquarters was, I'd be shot. I would be foolish to risk my life for criminals. Tell him where the partisans were, then I'd be free to return to my home and loved ones. I begged him to believe I was telling the truth. If I knew where the partisans were, I absolutely would tell him. I didn't want to die!

He stood. His expression changed abruptly, as if a switch had been thrown. His face darkened. At that moment, I knew I was in a cage in Hell. He commanded me to empty my pockets and put everything on the table. Hardly able to control my shaking hands, I took out my wallet, a small, unmarked bottle of aspirin, change, and a handkerchief. He glanced at my "belongings" then he ordered me to open my fly.

The instant he saw my circumcision he went crazy. He pushed over his chair, jumped up from behind the desk, and came toward me like a maniac. He swung his fists wildly, punching me in the head and face, wherever he could reach. I collapsed on the floor, unconscious. When I opened my eyes, he was standing over me screaming, "Damned dirty Jew! Damned dirty Jew! Damned dirty Jew! Damned dirty Jew!" He kicked me in the jaw with his boot, knocking out several teeth. I lay there bleeding, in racking pain, barely conscious. Hardly able to move my bloody, broken mouth, I asked the interpreter to tell the officer I wasn't a Jew.

"If you're not a Jew, how come you're circumcised?" Even in agony, the instinct to survive produces a ready response. I told him I had a venereal disease. That's why I had the pills. The doctor told me to stay on medication. The Untersturmfuhrer said to the interpreter, sarcastically, "Tell the damn dog not only is the bastard dog a Jew but on top of that he's a chronic syphilitic." They laughed. It was their kind of humor. The Untersturmfuhrer kicked me in the groin. "That should help your condition, dog." They enjoyed that one, too.

I knew I couldn't endure much more. I told the interpreter to tell the officer if he didn't believe me to shoot me. "Why did he have to torture me like this? Get it over with. Just kill me."

"Be patient Jew dog, it won't be long," the Untersturmfuhrer shot back.

He picked up my wallet and began rifling through it. Out fell the picture of the Virgin Mary that Ludovit Argay's mother had given me. I remembered her counsel, "Always carry it. She will protect you and bring you luck" The Untersturmfuhrer stopped and studied it. He put it back into my wallet and threw it at me with the rest of my belongings. "Get up dog. Get out." I could hardly move. I stuffed everything in my pocket, lifted myself up and stumbled back to our room. I don't know how long I laid on the floor in a daze.

After the Untersturmfuhrer finished with my two remaining companions, the five of us were loaded into a truck and driven to Banska Bystrica, fifteen miles west. Each jarring rut in the amply pitted dirt road shot a bolt of pain through me. We were taken to a jail and thrown into a cell with no window and one bucket. We were intensely hungry but too mentally and physically spent to think about when, if at all, we'd get our next meal. The others fell asleep almost at once. I was able to doze only off and on. My head pulsated with pain. Penetrating cold from the dank, dirt floor made the throb piercing.

I must have eventually drifted off because I wasn't aware that anyone had come into the cell until four soldiers stood over us shouting, "Raus!" It was difficult to move. The cold had stiffened my joints. We were marched through the streets, stumbling through the blackness. I had no doubt that this time I had just minutes to live. They were taking us to be shot, I was sure of it. Again, I had to reconcile myself to dying. Later, I learned my premonition was correct. The Germans' modus operandi was to load "enemies of the state" into trucks, take them to a quarry outside town and shoot them.

Suddenly, an air raid siren pierced the dead quiet.

The guards, obviously startled themselves, pushed us toward a nearby shelter. One of them shouted that the shelter is for Germans, civilians weren't allowed in it. We were near a railroad yard. They shoved us toward a row box cars parked on a siding. They unbolted the door of the first car they came to and threw us into the mass of people locked inside. "Don't go away, we'll be back for you," one soldier sniggered.

The box car was pitch dark. Trying to maneuver, I heard the curses of people I couldn't keep from stepping on. My mouth hurt too much to keep saying, "Sorry." When my eyes grew accustomed to the darkness, I could see a hundred, or so, ragged civilians crammed together. There was standing room only.

It was hard to decide which was worse during that eternity in the box car: waiting to be shot; waiting to be bombed; or the gagging stench from those wretched, inanimate, people. Suddenly, the train lurched and moved backward coasting for several seconds before it jolted to a halt.

From inside the car, the siren sounding All Clear was faint. I had heard no explosions. The raid must have been elsewhere. I tried sliding the door open. It didn't budge. I heard shouting at a distance, "You five Slovaks, Raus! Raus!" Our guards had returned for us. When they saw we weren't where they expected us to be, there was a commotion. Box car doors slid open and slammed shut. Everyone in earshot heard that prisoners had escaped. Five Slovak partisans were on the loose. Someone in authority wanted to know what was going on? Shouting, apparently at the guards, he demanded to know who gave them permission to put prisoners in a box car? No one was permitted near those cars. An argument followed until the one in authority screamed, "Enough!" He had a military supply train to dispatch. The box cars had to be moved immediately to make way. There was no time for a search. Still arguing, the voices faded off.

Soon after, our train lurched again. Instead of coasting, it gradually picked up speed. We weren't being repositioned, we were being transported. Glancing at the forlorn assortment of pitiful souls around me, I doubted it was to any place pleasant.

Chapter 9

The Camp

God is quirky. Or is it fate? No longer was I certain. On our way to execution an air raid warning sounds. Guards toss us into a box car for "safe-keeping," while they sit out the raid in a shelter. For some reason, the box car is shunted down the siding, far enough to disorient the guards when they come looking for us after the All Clear. Before they can find us, our train is dispatched to make way for a supply train going to the front. Had it not been for that chance air raid warning and the distance of several yards I would be facing a firing squad. I still might be. But for the time being, I had a reprieve.

I was cramped on the floor, my face swollen, my jaw throbbing. I had caught a cold that was worsening. I had a fever that was rising. I was miserable. But I was alive!

I learned that those in the box car had been taken by the Germans to keep them from helping the Russians. No one knew where the train was headed except that it was obviously going west.

All night the train travelled by fits and starts. It slowed, speeded up, slowed again, then stopped in the middle of nowhere. It got underway only to travel a short distance then stand for hours in a station whose sign showed, to the little relief I could muster, that we were still on Slovak soil.

Around me everyone was asleep, snoring in guttural discord. I envied their temporary escape from the dread of what lay ahead. I tried willing myself to sleep. I couldn't shut down my mind, terrified about what awaited me at the end of the line. Despite all, I took some comfort from the security of a large group and the anonymity it provided. I realized that the sense of vulnerability diminishes in proportion to the number of people around you in the same predicament. I just had to keep my wits about me and my covenant concealed.

Before daybreak the train started moving again. Hardly anyone noticed, the snoring continued without abatement. I wondered how they could breath so deeply without gagging on the reeking stench of their filth and waste? An hour or so after first light we pulled into another station. The sign was in German: "Eggenburg." I didn't know it then, but we were in Austria.

The train continued on a few more hours until it reached a small station and shunted to a siding. I couldn't see the station sign. German soldiers ordered everyone out of the car and into a compound enclosed by barbed wire. Hundreds of soldiers and civilians were milling about. It looked like a military camp. There were barracks, a field kitchen, and a detail of soldiers marching somewhere.

We were herded to the field kitchen. The Germans were providing the food, getting containers to hold it was our problem. I ran to a pile of trash and rifled through it. I found a grimy, rusting, Norwegian sardine can. Holding the can by the key still wrapped in it, I wiped it out with dead grass and shuffled into line. I had eaten almost nothing in two and half harrowing days. I was starving. With the prospect of a meal I forgot my cold, fever, and throbbing pain, for the time being anyway. The ladler considered me sympathetically. With my dirty clothes, caked nose, and unshaved, swollen face, I undoubtedly looked the way I felt. He dug deep in the kettle to find more of the solids that had settled to the bottom of the watery soup. To this day I still have a fondness for Norwegian sardine cans.

We remained in the camp overnight, outside in the cold on the bare ground. The five of us from the bunker stayed together, huddling against one another for warmth. In the morning, we were loaded back into the train with one fresh bucket in each box car. I was lucky, during the night the soup had worked its way through my system so I was able to relieve myself in the empty, dark, latrine without fear of someone noticing my covenant. After the frosty night outdoors, my cold and fever were worse but for some reason the pain in my jaw had lessened.

We travelled a roundabout route, heading in various directions. Through the slits in the box car I saw station signs appear, then reappear. We went one way, then another, only to have to double back to find a continuous course to get wherever we were going. The constant Allied bombings had left the rail system in chaos. The Germans worked round-the-clock trying to replace destroyed track. In one station, a locomotive was sitting on the roof of the station house. It was satisfying to see the awesome destructive force of an Allied bombing raid.

We were in that cold, filthy train without food a full day and night before it came to the final stop at dawn on a bleak, frigid early December morning, the sixth since our capture. It was a Sunday. Another Sunday.

A German soldier shoved open the box car door, ordering us out, quickly. Despite the cold, the blast of fresh air felt good. It cleared the car's asphyxiating stench from my nostrils. Once the train was unloaded, it pulled out leaving several hundred ragged civilians standing in front of some kind of camp.

Inside the open gate were rows and rows of barracks, many destroyed, amid a few squat buildings. A tall, barbed wire fence surrounded the muddy grounds. Despite the camp's size, I saw only a few inmates meandering about. I saw no guard towers or German soldiers. No one paid any attention to us. No one had even met the train. I had no idea where we were. The only place to go was into the camp, nothing else was in sight.

The guards from the train herded us toward the gate. The group picked up speed until they were running like unfettered sheep. I joined the rush wondering what I was heading into. The mob ran to a row of empty, damaged barracks to stake their claims to shelters.

Mato and I decided to stick together. We liked each other, knew we could depend upon each other and, most important to me, I felt my secret was reasonably safe with him. Our three other bunker-mates had gone their separate ways with acquaintances they met on the train.

It was against my interest to make new acquaintances. A new acquaintance meant questions: where did I come from; where did I work; am I married; do I have children; how'd I get caught? The more I talked, the more I risked making a slip. The instant anyone found out I was a Jew, I was doomed. Germans weren't the only anti-Semites around. At the same time, I needed human contact, someone to talk to, commiserate with, and help me if I needed it. Emotionally and psychologically, being alone in that situation was unwise. I was lucky to have Mato.

We found a barracks with most of its windows blown out. The building was narrow with a long hallway that entered into about two dozen small, open cubicles. Several people had already claimed the cubicles toward the middle of the barracks. They were cramped into the tiny rooms huddled on crudely made beds of straw to help insulate themselves against the cold. They had found the straw outside. Mato and I staked out a cubicle at the end of the barracks figuring that being in a corner of the building would provide better protection against the weather. Mato held the corner while I brought in the straw. We sat on our "beds" bewildered, waiting for we knew not what. Still, no one from the camp paid attention to us.

It was mid-afternoon. I went outside to find out when we'd be fed. I learned there was no food in the camp. It was brought in from outside because air raids had put the camp's kitchen building out of commission. There'd be no food until next day. I returned to the barracks depressed, hurting, hungry, and so exhausted that I fell into a deep sleep until early the next morning when I woke up with a start.

Someone was in the hallway shouting, in German, "I will have all the Slovaks shot!" Though they didn't understand what he said, the frenzy in his voice alarmed everyone in the barracks. It terrified me. I had understood. We moved cautiously, poking our heads into the hallway to see what was happening. A rail-thin man in civilian clothes demanded to know who gave us dumb Slovaks permission to take the straw? We just stood there. This made him all the angrier. I sensed that things would get worse if no one spoke up. To me his rage was an overreaction. I figured the man was angry at us because he had wanted the straw for himself. He hardly impressed me as anyone in authority. In fact, just the opposite. Standing there so fragile looking and in civilian clothes, I thought he was another inmate.

By reflex, I asked in German who he was and what was he carrying on about? He stared at me. "You will find out who I am soon enough," he said. His stare remained fixed, but his expression became studied. Instantly and with sinking heart, I knew I had made a critical blunder. I could have torn out my tongue. I had drummed it into my head never to speak German as long as I carried Aryan papers. To do so indicated that as a Slovak I was also probably a Jew. By inadvertently uttering that one sentence in German, I had imperiled my so far successful guise as a Gentile. By speaking up, I had also lost anonymity. One sentence and the course of my destiny changed, yet again.

Already, my fate had turned on chance several times. Except for the U.S. consul's decision not to overlook an insignificant technicality and approve my visa to America, I had been lucky, so far. When I chose the least of three possible career evils and became a lumberman instead of a rabbi or a lawyer; when greed was more important to the Greek Orthodox priest and Slovak border guard than commitment to God and country and I lost only my money in the baptismal certificate scam; when a newspaper story forewarned me about the danger of attempting an escape to Switzerland in a box car of charcoal; when I had the premonition about the first mass roundup in May 1942 and sought sanctuary at Frau Kesselbauer's; when I received the life-saving phone call from an unknown savior alerting me to the last major roundup of Jews in Presov; when Ludovit Argay's mother gave me the picture of the Virgin Mary for good luck and I had the good sense to keep it; when the air raid siren sounded as I was being marched to be shot; when the train I had been thrown into during the air raid shunted a few critical yards, yet far enough to take me from death's clutch. Now, after all I had been through, to make the stupid, perhaps, fatal mistake of speaking in German. How long could my luck hold out?

"You speak German," the skinny civilian asked. He

had heard me so how could I tell him no? "A little," I replied timorously.

"Then you will translate for me." He shouted, "Tell those dumb Slovaks to pick up every bit of straw and throw it back where they found it. It's infested with lice. It was put outside to be burned. Raus!" We found out later that typhus had broken out in the camp a few weeks before and all the straw was ordered burned.

The man commanded me to follow him to each barracks of new Slovak arrivals to translate. On the way, I screwed up enough courage to ask him when we would get some food. "Soon," he snapped. After making his rounds, he dismissed me and disappeared.

An hour later, a truck rumbled in with the food contained in large cans. It was like seeing the cavalry arrive. It took no time for word to spread among the new arrivals and the mad dash to the dispensing tables set up in front of old camp kitchen building was on. Dreadful as the soup tasted, it was my first meal in two days and it was warm. I savored it as if it were a delicacy.

Each daily food shipment included that evening's meal and the next morning's breakfast. Supper was a scoop of slush with strands of shredded beets, potatoes, and cabbage. Breakfast consisted of two slices of bread and luke-warm tea. Apparently, the food cans were insulated. It wasn't much of a diet. It never satisfied our hunger but, at least, we were eating regularly. It was a discomfiting way to learn the difference between hunger and starvation.

After the meal, we returned to our barracks. A short while later, another civilian poked his head into our cubicle and said the camp commandant wanted to see me. My stomach knotted. Speaking German had raised a suspicion about me, I was sure of it. The man walked briskly. I staggered after him trying to keep my balance. "What does the commandant want with me," I gasped.

"Don't know. He just ordered me find the German-speaking Slovak." What little I had in my bowel let go.

Camp headquarters was a small, nondescript, wooden building with an anteroom and an office. The office was spare and not much larger than my cubicle in the barracks. Behind the desk sat a man wearing, incongruously, an everyday shirt, no tie, a sweater, and military breeches and boots. It was the skinny civilian from that morning.

"You stink!"

Stammering, I apologized, explaining that I hadn't washed or changed clothes in almost a week. "You must get a bath immediately," he said, friendlier. "I want you to be the translator at registration. I held onto the desk to keep from collapsing with relief. He called out a name. In came a boy who couldn't have been more than fifteen. He ordered the boy to fetch a can of coals and bring them to the kitchen. "Your name," the commandant asked.

"Ludovit Argay, sir."

"Ludovit has to take a bath," he said to the boy. Then waving his hand in front of his nose, he added, "He stinks." The camp commandant pointed to the old kitchen building only a few hundred feet away. "You will fix your bath in there." As I started to go, he said wait. Again, I felt that twinge of apprehension. What next? He opened his desk drawer, took out a razor and handing it to me, said, "And shave, too, you look like a bum. You have to look presentable."

On my way to the old kitchen, intoxicated with relief and the prospect of a bath, the realization that I was in mortal danger brought me up short. My covenant! I ran to the barracks to fetch Mato. I told him about the bath and the problem. I bargained that if he stood watch while I bathed he could have a bath, too.

We dumped coal into an open hearth, lit a fire and

filled a hundred gallon kettle with pails of water we pumped in back of building. As much as I wanted to linger in the warm, soothing bath, I washed quickly. Even with Mato standing watch, it was foolish to take unnecessary chances. I already had made the mistake of speaking German. It seemed a fortunate blunder at that time but it could backfire and be my undoing. After Mato bathed we shaved and washed our clothes in the dirty water. Except for the hunger, I hadn't felt as good in a long time. I was clean, my cold and fever were breaking, and my jaw ached only slightly. The rest of the day I relaxed and rested.

Registration did not take place until the following morning. Apparently our arrival came as a surprise to the camp commandant, which had not made him happy. Aside from the additional logistical headaches it caused him, he needed time to arrange for a staff to handle the paper work.

At registration, a dozen female clerks sat at long tables in a large hall near the camp headquarters. In front of each girl was a large ledger and an ink well. I was posted nearby to handle whatever translation they could not.

They were as curious about me as I was about them. They wanted to know where I had come from, how close the Russians were, how the war was going. They couldn't get accurate information from the German press, of course, though they were not about to say as much.

From them, I learned that they all were German nationals from Hungary, Rumania, and Poland who had fled the Russians. I also found out where we were. It was a labor camp near Augsburg, a city of roughly two hundred thousand people, forty miles northwest of Munich. The camp was assigned to the Messerschmitt airplane factory, two miles away, on the outskirts of the city from which the camp took its name. Augsburg was a subsidiary camp of a main concentration center twenty miles to the southeast: Dachau. Jews and political prisoners were sent there. Slave labor went to Augsburg. At the time, the name "Dachau" meant nothing.

The camp commandant had been severely wounded on the eastern front. After recuperating, he was mustered out of the army and given the privilege of continuing his service to the Fatherland at Augsburg. He was not only thin but sallow and sick-looking.

Registration for the four hundred fifty Slovaks who had arrived on the train two days before took only a few hours. All the clerks wanted to know was: name, birth date, and where we came from. No other information was needed because the camp charged Messerschmitt for labor sent to the factory on a per head basis. Anything beyond a few vital statistics was unnecessary.

That night we got new blankets and straw for mattresses. Still, we needed each other's closeness for warmth. I fell asleep dreaming about the breakfast waiting in the large cans only a few hundred yards away.

The next two days we spent sleeping, drifting around the camp, and looking forward to the next meal. Our first day on the job, we were roused at five in the morning in the dark and cold. There were no roll calls in the camp. We received our two slices of bread and tea, directed to the Messerschmitt plant, and ordered on our way. As we walked like zombies, half asleep, I kept looking for the guards. There were none. Only a grumpy civilian was at the head of the column to show us the way. I was astounded that the Germans allowed us to walk the two miles unescorted.

The idea of escape went through my mind as I'm sure it did everyone else's. But where would I go? How far could I get in the cold with no food and no money?

Who would help an escaped prisoner or take me in looking the way I did, like a bum in rags, especially in Germany? In other countries, civilians did what they could to help victims of the hated Nazis. But to the patriotic German populace, anyone on the run was considered either an enemy of the state or a traitor. The likelihood of being reported and caught was too great to chance. Once in the Gestapo's hands, they would open my fly and that would be that. I continued walking.

It had snowed overnight. As it grew light, rising temperatures turned the snow into slush which made the going exhausting. It hardly helped that my shoes were soaked-through and my wet feet were freezing.

Approaching the Messerschmitt factory through the outskirts of Augsburg, seeing the widespread destruction from Allied bombing lifted my spirits. It was early, the few people in the streets ignored us. When we reached the factory, I was baffled. Except for a small section in tact at the near end, most of it was in ruins. The plant wasn't operational. What work could there be for us here?

A few German soldiers came out of the near end of the building. One told us what we were to do: take bricks from the piles of rubble strewn about, scrape them clean, and stack the cleaned bricks neatly. They handed out picks for the job.

We set to work without supervision. No one paid attention to us. If we cleaned three bricks or three hundred bricks a day no one took a count or seemed to care. I learned that the cleaned bricks were to be reused. For what, was a good question. The Germans had all they could do to survive let alone think about rebuilding. Maybe our work assignment was simply a way to get several hundred people out of the camp administration's hair each day. I didn't complain, it was easy work. No one bothered us, though life was by no means relaxed.

Every waking moment there was the relentless hunger. You can condition yourself to almost anything but hunger.

Day after day throughout the winter, the routine never varied: up at five a.m.; two slices of bread and tea; trudge the two miles to the Messerschmitt factory in the brutal morning cold, which an issue of wooden shoes made agonizing to our frost-bitten feet; clean bricks outdoors all day; get only a half hour break at midday for a lunch of sugar-beet slush and bread; drag ourselves back to the camp in the pitch dark, exhausted; devour another portion of slush for supper; lie on our mattresses of straw in the damp, cold night waiting for merciful sleep and cope with lice.

From time to time, there were slight breaks in the routine and boredom, but never enough to blunt my hunger or the fear of discovery. Occasionally, instead of cleaning bricks at the Messerschmitt factory, the camp commandant assigned me to do translation for sick Slovaks who remained in the camp for treatment. Or an inmate would find a German newspaper and bring it to our barracks for me to translate. It provided evening entertainment. Reading between the lines, the news had a favorable effect on morale. The "heroic" German armies were winning or holding their own on every front, even though the battlefields were getting ever closer to Berlin. The almost nightly air raid warnings also fueled hope, but having to hustle into the shallow trenches, called shelters, was one break from routine I could have done without. It was only during air raids that we were kept under guard. Smoking or lighting a match was strictly forbidden lest it be seen from the air.

Prisoners were free to circulate among barracks but most didn't. They were suspicious of strangers. Undoubtedly, the different nationalities and language barriers had something to do with the mutual distrust. The camp had become a dumping ground for refugees, not only Slovaks, but Hungarians, Rumanians, Czechs, Dutch, French, Belgians, and even a few Australian soldiers. One Australian used to visit our barracks to talk with me. Except for his countrymen, few in the camp spoke English. Once, when I felt poorly, he brought me figs in milk from his Red Cross package which he received once a month.

The overwhelming majority of inmates were men. The few women inmates circulated with relative freedom around the camp, more to barter for food and cigarettes than to be sociable. They willingly traded their special "currency" for the extra rations. There was always a private corner handy to exchange trade.

Because I spoke Hungarian, a Hungarian girl took a liking to me. Despite being very thin (who wasn't), her face still held some allure. She did me little favors such as cleaning out my canteen, tidying my straw, scrubbing my wooden shoes. She made it clear that she wanted more than a simple friendship. After so many months without a woman, so did I. My ration of ten cigarettes a week increased my appeal to her even more. I didn't smoke so either I used the cigarettes to barter for food or gave them to Mato. For a few cigarettes, she would do anything I wanted but I was afraid to touch her. Getting involved meant exposing my covenant. How long it had been since I had last touched, or hugged, or loved another human being? As desperately as I wanted that woman, I had to break off the relationship. I found out later it was just as well. She was pregnant and looking for someone to latch on to. Even in those convulsive times, being pregnant and unwed was a disgrace.

As grim as life was, it was not without its lighter moments. One night we were fed soup with bits of meat in it. Its rich brown color made the soup even look appetizing. The meat tasted funny but we attributed it to our not having had meat for so long that we forgot how it tasted. It didn't take long for the mad dash to the latrines to start. Those, like me, who had to wait for a place and were too sick to hold on let go in our pants. It wasn't long before the latrines, which were waterless holes in the ground, filled and overflowed onto the wooden planks between the barracks that led to the latrines. Traction decreased as traffic increased. People slipped and slid trying to keep their balance. A number were unsuccessful and fell. In their frenzy to stand up, with hands, face, and clothes covered, some reached their feet only to fall into the muck again. Despite the severe diarrhea and incredible reeking stench and filth, in a warped way, the scene was hilarious.

Though it took a few days for the toxin to pass its way out of our systems, most workers were back on the job the next morning. Word had it that those declaring themselves very sick often didn't return. As the weeks passed and malnutrition increased the amount of sickness in the camp, the number of inmates declined noticeably.

My job as translator for the commandant began to take up more and more of my time. So much so that we gradually developed a rapport. He became almost cordial. He was interested in where I lived, what I did for a living, was I married, did I have children, and so on.

One day near the end of February, I decided to chance finding out the extent of our rapport. I had a scheme. I suggested he increase food rations for the Slovaks. I told him that unless he did, sickness in the camp was bound to get even worse and, with it, so would worker productivity. I pointed out that Slovaks and Germans were allies and we couldn't help our mutual cause if we were too weak to work. He agreed but said with food shortages everywhere, his superiors were unlikely to approve extra rations for his camp just because he requested it. I suggested making the appeal to the Slovak government, let Slovaks feed Slovaks. The country was still a productive food producer, despite the war. It was their obligation to protect its people. I asked the commandant if he would mind my drafting a letter to the Slovak consul in Berlin. To my great surprise he readily agreed. I sensed he was thinking that if he pulled off the plan, it would look very good in his record. He even let me use the typewriter in his office.

Drafting the letter, I felt like two people. And in a way, I was. Memories of another typewriter in another office on Hlinkova Street flooded back. It was hard to relate that other person in that other life to the skeletal, lice-ridden, ragged remnant who sat at that typewriter in the Augsburg slave labor camp.

I wrote:

> Dear Honorable Ambassador:
>
> I am turning to you in the name of all Slovak workers who were transported to this camp. More than four hundred of us are foundering.
>
> I don't want to make unreasonable requests, since we know the difficulties it would create. We want only that you try to ease our plight here in Augsburg. We were deported here without clothing and other essentials. We have lice. Worst of all, we have little food. We do not wish to lose our moral and spiritual enthusiasm. We are not derelicts. We are decent people who would like to show our allies that we cherish order, cleanliness, and our common cause.
>
> We cannot demonstrate anything without proper nourishment. Without essential needs. Therefore, we are turning to you, honorable consul, with a request that you somehow arrange that some of what is rightfully ours be forwarded from Bratislava.
>
> We do not wish to be a bother or dictate how you should help us. But we are in distress and are appealing to

> you as our protector. We strongly hope that you will fulfill our request for help speedily.
>
> Other foreign nationals in the camp receive help via Red Cross packages containing food and other essentials.
>
> We especially ask that our request be given preferential treatment and not be bogged down in the bureaucracy.
>
> We would be very happy if someone from the embassy would visit us and see for themselves that we are without shoes and essential needs.
>
> I close begging you to excuse my writing on such inferior paper but it is the best at my disposal. I also ask understanding for troubling you in these difficult times. We wouldn't do it if we saw any other possibility.
>
> In anticipation of your prompt response, we remain with feelings of gratitude and hope for our return to our homeland soon, your fellow Slovaks.We close with our national greeting-
>
> **On Guard!**

Word of the letter quickly got around. To the Slovaks in the camp I became a minor hero. They were proud that I had taken such an initiative. Each night during supper and in my barracks a parade of people came by asking the same question: "Had I heard anything?"

One day, after two weeks had passed with no reply to the letter, the camp commandant sent for me. My first thought was that he had heard something. He had, but it wasn't from the Slovak consul in Berlin. The chief administrator at the Messerschmitt plant had called ordering me to report to him at once. I asked if he knew why. He didn't. The administrator said only that he had some questions he wanted to ask me. I thought, "That's it. They have found out I'm a Jew."

After I left the camp commandant's office, I just

made it to the latrine. Had someone been there, with my urgency so great, I honestly don't know what I would have done about protecting my covenant.

I went to the Messerschmitt factory alone, without a guard. I thought about escaping, trying to make it to the Swiss border, about a hundred miles away. As I had each time I considered escape, I concluded that there were too many obstacles. I had no money. I was physically weak. Even if I were strong enough, I wouldn't have been able to walk very far in my wooden shoes. The way I looked and smelled, infested with lice, the chance of getting enough help along the way was remote. And with the shortages and bombings, the people had all they could do for themselves to survive from day to day. There was always the likelihood of being reported or being spotted by police, or worse, by the Gestapo or SS. I wasn't certain why I had been called but the odds of my surviving seemed better by reporting to the factory administrator, than by attempting to escape.

Before I was taken into his office, I had to sign a paper pledging not to repeat anything I saw or heard. Stamped on the paper was the warning, "Psst, the enemy is listening, too."

I was brought into the presence of a Wehrmacht officer, Oberleutnant Treuer. He was tall but not imposing, with pleasant features that were more those of a gentleman than a soldier. We shook hands. Politely, he asked me to sit. I was still apprehensive. I had been through the routine before. He began. "Mr. Argay, I called you here because we have a problem." I thought, "This is finally it." He took an official looking document from a folder. It had the Nazi emblem stamped at the top: the eagle holding the swastika in its talons. "We have a Slovak in the plant who looks to us to be Jewish. He has Jewish tendencies. Somehow he has illegally obtained ration tickets for soap and he's selling them in the plant." When I realized the officer wasn't after me, it was like snapping out of a drugged state. I sat up alert. I wanted to shout from relief!

When he told me the Slovak's name, I said that I didn't know the man personally but knew of him. Then I added, inventing somewhat, that my parents had known his parents and they were not Jewish. He asked if there were many Jews where we lived. I replied, "yes, but they were all taken away." The Oberleutnant said that with so many Jews in his midst, the Slovak must have acquired his Jewish mentality without being aware of it. After all, a Jew's ways were so insidious it was easy to understand how they could infect a person caught unaware. I couldn't believe my ears. Oberleutnant Treuer was protecting the Slovak. My confusion was soon cleared up. He called out a name. From an adjoining room in walked a civilian with the Nazi Party pin in his lapel. He was the ever-present Party man always on the prowl to ferret out subversive activity against the Fuerher and the Fatherland.

Treuer explained to the man that he had questioned Mr. Argay thoroughly and Mr. Argay assured him that the soap marketeer is not Jewish. "You see," Treuer added, "I told you there were no Jews here." The Party man shook his head and left.

As I stood to go Treuer asked, off-hand, how I was faring in the camp? During our conversation, I had gotten the impression, despite his blind-spot about Jews (who knew how many years he had been indoctrinated with anti-Semitic claptrap), that Oberleutnant Treuer was a basically decent man. Nothing like his counterparts in the SS. I felt comfortable with him. I decided to take the chance and respond to his perfunctory question.

I told him about our meager rations and the letter I sent to the Slovak consul in Berlin, adding that, as yet, we hadn't received a reply. He said I wouldn't because the consul wasn't in Berlin, he was in Munich. I asked for the address so I could write another letter. Treuer suggested that instead of wasting precious time sending a letter, I should see the consul in person. He would take care of the paperwork.

I was dumfounded. I didn't want to go to Munich. I wanted nothing to do with exposing myself to such a danger: conducting official business with my time bomb between my legs. I tried to talk myself out of the mission, asking him to take a good look at me. In my condition and appearance did I look like a suitable emissary? Surely there were others more qualified and refined than I.

He replied that no one looked good these days; that from the way I expressed myself, obviously I had education; that because I was a common man and a Slovak there was a strong chance the consul would listen to me; that the whole thing was my idea in the first place. He said to come back in two days. He had to get consent for the mission from his superiors. Walking back to the camp, I decided such a bizarre scheme hadn't a chance for approval. The thought relieved me, but only a little.

That night, I went to see the Slovak about whom Oberleutnant Treuer had questioned me. I told him to be careful, the Germans were wise to what he was doing. Then I said, "Today I saved your life. I don't know if you are Jewish or not and I don't care. But if you are a Jew, you have to be the dumbest Jew I've ever met in my life. The war is almost over. You've made it this far. And you're so reckless that you jeopardize your life to sell ration stamps in the Messerschmitt factory right under the Germans' noses." From then on, I made sure to avoid him for fear of being linked to him in any way.

Two days later, Oberleutnant Treuer sent for me. He handed me the written order authorizing Ludovit Argay to go to Munich on 19 March 1945-the next day-for a hearing with the Slovak consul and return the same day. He handed me money for the train ticket and ration stamps for food. I was to leave first thing in the morning.

In the barracks that night I asked myself repeatedly, "What had I gotten myself into? What the hell was I doing? How could I get out of such a mad mission?" There was no way out.

I ruminated about how crazy fate was. The Germans were sending a Jew on a diplomatic mission to the Slovak consul to assist the administrators of a German slave labor camp in relieving their food shortage to make it easier to maintain their war quotas. It was hair-raising. I spent much of the night in the latrine. The rest of the time I wondered what fate had in store for me in Munich.

Chapter 10

Missions

Each day you survived was a singular victory. You considered yourself a hero. Existence, already wretched, was getting worse. The cold, the lice, the incessant fear of discovery, the hunger, were wearing me away. I once carried one hundred ninety five pounds on a six-feet, one-inch, frame. In three months, forty five of those pounds were gone. My bones seemed to outweigh the rest of me.

Still, demented as it was, compared to life as a fugitive on the run, wondering every day if it would be my last; compared to the brutality of capture, with death so close at hand; life in the camp for all its wretchedness had a certain tranquility. The camp had become an unlikely sanctuary from torment and cruelty, from the ceaseless terror of being the fox futilely trying to escape the hounds. Now, suddenly, the fox had been forced back into the chase, heading toward another mortal danger.

I got up early to cover the few miles from the camp to the train station in Augsburg by 7:00 a.m. I cleaned up as best I could. The night before I had given my clothes a cold-water wash under the water pump outside the barracks. No amount of scrubbing could budge the ingrained grime from my threadbare clothes. As for the lice, creatures no larger than a bread crumb, soaping myself only moved them around. They crawled and bit at will. They were impossible to shake loose. They buried themselves into my hair and burrowed into my skin. They were tough to get at and even tougher to kill.

The train had standing room only. Mostly civilians were on board looking as shabby as I. It took two hours to make the forty mile trip. Unable to see out of the windows, the ride seemed even longer. Mercifully, it was also uneventful.

The main train station in Munich was operational and bustling with people despite its considerable damage. I asked directions to the Slovak consulate. It turned out to be only a short distance from the station, but the constant detours around the debris that was everywhere turned the walk into a forty minute hike. There was little activity in the streets. Most buildings had been severely damaged or destroyed.

When I reached the street where the Slovak consulate was located, the corner street sign to point me in the right direction was sticking out of the rubble. I didn't know which way to go, not that it would have made any difference. As far as I could see in either direction, most buildings were in ruin. I considered ending my lunatic mission and heading back to the camp. I'd tell Oberleutnant Treuer that the consulate had been destroyed and the consul was nowhere to be found. I quickly scrapped the idea as not being too bright. Treuer's obvious reaction would be to question why I hadn't asked someone where the consul had moved. Then he'd probably send me back to Munich to find out.

I approached an old man in a tattered air-raid warden's uniform and asked him if this was the street where the Slovak consulate was located. He motioned toward the middle of the block, pointing to a pile of rubble and caustically replied, "There." The man's drawn, careworn face expressed hostility and disillusion. He said he didn't know where the Slovak consulate had moved. I could find out at Gestapo headquarters only a few blocks away. He gave me directions then walked away slowly without another word.

I stood there. "What do I do now," I asked myself. My mission to the Slovak consul was frightening enough, now I was faced with deciding whether to walk into the most fearsome building in the city.

As I debated what to do, I found myself walking in the direction of Gestapo headquarters. Several times I passed back and forth outside the grated iron fence that enclosed the large yard at the side of the building. The structure, which had sustained considerable damage, was a massive building in red brick. A guard booth stood at the back of the yard near the entrance to the building which faced away from the street. The way the entrance was situated, I could see little activity. As I paced outside the fence, I tried to weigh the pros and cons of the almost Solomonian dilemma I faced. If I went in, the risks were obvious. But I was carrying an official order from Messerschmitt that should help to put me beyond suspicion. It was also in my favor that no one would think a Jew had the temerity, to say nothing of the stupidity, to walk into Gestapo headquarters. If I did not go in, there was the good chance that Oberleutnant Treuer would send me back. I decided to go ahead with the mission reasoning that one way or the other I'd have to deal with Gestapo headquarters and better to get it over with now. It all came down to the realization that I couldn't go through this trauma again.

The decision made, I continued to pace outside the fence. A few Gestapo officials in their long black leather coats and some SS were milling about in the yard. Seeing them turned my fear into terror. I couldn't bring myself to walk through the gate, I didn't think my legs would carry me past them to the guard booth. I took a long walk around the block. When I reached the front gate again, the yard was empty. I told myself, "This is it. It's now or never."

Slowly, I walked the several yards down the pathway to the guard booth. The SS soldier came outside and put up his hand for me to halt. In my disheveled appearance, I knew that I hardly looked like someone on an official mission. Before he could size me up or ask intimidating questions, I saluted "Heil Hitler," explained why I was there, and showed him the order from Messerschmitt. He directed me to go inside the building and see the guard at the desk at the head of the hallway.

A huge Nazi flag waved above the entry way. It was an effort climbing the stone steps. Inside, Gestapo and SS were industriously going about their business. No one paid any attention to me. Standing there, I was tempted to look around but kept my eyes staring straight ahead for fear of doing anything that might draw attention to me.

The guard at the desk sent me to an office down the hallway. Saluting "Heil Hitler" to the secretary, I showed her my order and explained my problem. She said she didn't know the whereabouts of the Slovak consul. I should try another office on the second floor, maybe I could find out there. So, in a trance, I climbed the stairway, going deeper into the tiger's cage. In the second-floor office, I went through the same routine. An official told me the Slovak consul was no longer in Munich. He had moved to Vienna but didn't know the address. I said, "Danke," saluted "Heil Hitler," and left the building as quickly as I could.

That was it! I had been among the beasts and survived. I had seen the mission through. It was over! I could sit out the rest of the war inside the camp where, ironically, I felt more secure than I did on the outside. It was the end of March 1945, the war couldn't last much longer.

On the walk back to the train station, I was obviously relieved yet I also felt tension. The mission had failed. I became concerned about what might be in store next. Though fearful and preoccupied, I still had the presence of mind to remember the ration stamps Oberleutnant Treuer had given me. I went to a small restaurant and ate all the stamps could purchase: a bowl of real soup, with real meat and vegetables, and two slices of bread with margarine. It wasn't much but to me it was a feast.

I relaxed, taking my time. It struck me how true it was that fact was often stranger than fiction. Here I was a bloody Jew in a restaurant in Munich, the birthplace of Nazism, having a meal, after walking freely through Gestapo headquarters on a mission for Messerschmitt, the Reich's most important producer of war planes. So much for Nazi theory that "proved" the Jewish race had immutable identifying physical characteristics that not only were easily recognizable but justified its classification as sub-human.

When I returned to the camp that night the Slovaks were waiting for me as they would a returning hero. Surrounding me in the barracks, they couldn't wait to hear the good news, excitedly asking when the shipments of food would begin arriving? Seeing their hopefulness and exhilaration made what already had been an emotionally depleting mission more burdensome. After I recounted the day's events they dispersed slowly, disappointed and disconsolate.

The next morning, I made my report to the camp commandant. He agreed the results of my mission were disappointing but at least I had tried. He told me to go to the Messerschmitt plant and give the report to Oberleutnant Treuer. I felt relieved almost to the point of liberation.

Oberleutnant Treuer listened to the report without comment. When I finished, he praised my willingness to undertake the assignment and the good sense I showed going to Gestapo headquarters to find out the Slovak consul's whereabouts. He expressed disappointment that the mission had not succeeded, stressing how urgent it was to alleviate the scarcities in the camp. Then he said, matter-of-factly, "You'll have to go to Vienna." I had given my report standing. I sat without being asked, a breach of protocol. I couldn't keep my feet. My life had become a roller-coaster, plunging into and clambering out of crisis after crisis. Having just escaped one abyss, I was plummeting toward another.

I tried to collect my wits and think of a way out. Perhaps, an even more outrageous proposal than going to Vienna might do it. I suggested Bratislava be included in the same trip. I told Oberleutnant Treuer that seeing the Slovak consul in Vienna was certainly worthwhile but the official who really mattered was Sano Mach, the Interior Minister, who was in Bratislava. Besides, it is from Bratislava that the food would be shipped. To my chagrin, he liked the idea. He would take it to his superiors for approval.

The very next day the Oberleutnant ordered me to report to his office as soon as possible. Again-how often had it been-I felt that fearful jolt. Treuer undoubtedly wanted to see me about the mission, but there was always that grim possibility the Germans had found me out. In my wooden shoes, I tramped through the blustery March cold the two miles from the camp into the outskirts of Augsburg and to the idle Messerschmitt plant. I debated with myself, anew, the familiar question: to escape or not to escape. Again, I decided against it but for a reason that surprised me. I had taken a liking to Oberleutnant Treuer.

I was a prisoner, a slave laborer. Yet, he treated

me with respect and cordiality. In that darkest of times when human interaction was gruff and often brutal; when everyone was an enemy until proved otherwise and you avoided getting close enough to find out; when human dignity no longer existed; when life itself had become worthless; it was a medicament to hear a gentle voice, a congenial word. I was starved for affection. Any gesture of friendliness, any intimation of human warmth, no matter how slight, was a temporary deliverance from my continuing descent into the lower depths.

At the same time, I had no illusion that if Treuer discovered I was a Jew he would dispatch me without a second thought. I craved his kindliness more than I feared his duty to expunge his country's vilest enemy.

The Oberleutnant smiled as I was led into his office. He was delighted to inform me that his superiors had given their consent. However, they required more information about how I intended to carry out my plan. I was to appear before them the following morning to explain. He praised me for my intelligence and devotion to our common cause. He went on to make a short speech emphasizing how important that devotion was in such grave times. That we shouldn't give up. Yes, the ravages of bombing and transport disruptions had created serious food shortages. In fact, the Wehrmacht had orders to take no prisoners on the eastern front so as not to deplete food supplies. It was critical for Germans and Slovaks to continue working together, to hold the Allies at bay until the secret new weapons the Fuhrer promised were ready to be thrown into the war and turn the tide.

How desperately I must have hungered for Treuer's friendliness. His remarks repelled me, still I liked him. I excused his misguided patriotism as the product of years of propaganda and indoctrination. He had been kind to me. That kindness was more important than any scorn I might have had for him.

When I returned to the camp, I brought Mato up to date. He told me that he knew of an inmate, Jozef Bednarik, who was an acquaintance of Sano Mach, the Slovak Interior Minister. He said it may not be a bad idea to suggest to Treuer that Bednarik go along on the mission.

The next morning at the Messerschmitt plant, in a small conference room, with Hitler's picture above the entrance and swastikas on either wall, I faced Oberleutnant Treuer and three civilian officials. One was the Nazi party man who had been in Treuer's office the first time I was called into the Oberleutnant's presence. I learned later the two others were high officials in the Messerschmitt organization.

Nervously, I explained that as Slovaks it was the responsibility of our government to see to our welfare. An inmate I knew of in the camp was a friend of Slovakia's Interior Minister. The Minister was the authority who could best facilitate meeting our needs. Undoubtedly, our government would do all it could for our mutual benefit. Slovakia was an agricultural country with sufficient food supplies for the camp's several hundred Slovaks. We were entitled to rations in the camp the same as if we were still in Slovakia.

The party man asked me how I intended getting the food supplies from Bratislava to Augsburg. His tone suggested I hadn't considered that "small" matter. He was wrong. I told him the supplies would be loaded in railroad cars, we'd need only a few, and we'd have them painted with a red cross to deter bombing. Another official asked how long it would take for the supplies to reach Augsburg? I replied that, given the other priorities of war, I honestly didn't know. It was my guess, not more than three to four weeks. How could I make such an estimate, the party man challenged? I told him I had been a forester and was familiar with railroad procedures. I had overseen the loading and dispatching of charcoal to Switzerland and the shipments didn't take more than a few weeks from the time of departure to the time of arrival. I was allowing extra time in case the trains were temporarily diverted. Another official asked what kind of food I proposed to transport? I replied, nothing perishable, dried foods mostly, but I would leave that to the experts in Bratislava. They began murmuring among themselves, shaking their heads in assent. Out of the corner of my eye I saw that Oberleutnant looked pleased, the way a teacher proudly looks when his pupil has performed well. If I hadn't been so petrified standing before those high-ranking, influential Germans, I could have enjoyed the situation's dark humor and irony. Had they only known that Treuer's protegee and agent for the "grand plan" was a Jew.

Treuer walked me into the hallway, said he'd let me know their decision as soon as possible and returned to the meeting room. I prayed they would turn it down. It was incredible, but true, I was safer in the German work camp than I was in my own country. In the camp, I enjoyed the confidence of the camp commandant and the Messerschmitt factory administrator. I was beyond suspicion and treated like a virtual trustee. Sure, I had to keep vigilant about not accidentally exposing my covenant. But In Slovakia, I had that and more to worry about. There, I'd be a fugitive again. Worse, I could be recognized.

On the other hand, once I was in Bratislava I'd be less than three hundred miles from Presov, from home. Undoubtedly, the Russians had already liberated the area. How long it had been since I dared think of Presov, since I dared have any hope of ever seeing it again? I decided that if I went on the mission, I would never come back to Augsburg. I have often wondered if suggesting the addition of Bratislava to the travel plan was because of a subconscious desire to return to Slovakia, despite the dangers. It gave me the chance to reach home.

Word about the new mission had circulated around the camp and throughout the night expectant Slovaks came to see me for any news about the mission's approval, when I'd be leaving, when the food would be arriving, and with requests to look up relatives in Bratislava if I got the chance.

The day after the conference I was back in Oberleutnant Treuer's office. I had impressed the commission with my presentation and the wisdom of my plan. They had approved the mission to Vienna and Bratislava. I could take whom I wished but, unequivocally, he wanted me to head the delegation.

I told him I needed four others, explaining that with the inevitable bureaucracy we'd confront and the complex arrangements that were necessary, the more help I had the faster we'd accomplish our charge. Bednarik was an obvious choice because he knew the Interior Minister. Mato, of course. The two others were friends of Bednarik and Mato, respectively, Jan Longauer and Pavel Potacok. Treuer agreed without objection.

I asked about the necessary papers and other essentials. He said the official order, letters of introduction, train tickets, ration stamps, and three thousand crowns for the group would be ready before we departed.

Passports were another matter. We didn't have Slovak passports. He said the four of us should go to the Augsburg town hall next day and file for stateless passports. By international law, everyone is entitled to a passport including the stateless. He sent a clerk along with us to make sure a bureaucrat didn't encumber the paperwork. Treuer told us to be ready to depart in two days, March 23rd. He anticipated the mission would take no more than twenty one days. The order would be dated from 23 March 1945 through 12 April 1945.

The day before our departure, Treuer called me to his office. He wanted to wish me success on our undertaking and a safe return. I thanked him for being so supportive of the mission. I asked if there was anything I could bring back to him. Genuinely touched, he modestly requested some Meinl coffee and a walking cane.

Three years to the day of the first mass roundup of Slovak Jews and nine months after I had been forced to flee Presov, I was returning to Slovakia. As the five of us left camp for the train station, the cheers and well wishes of our fellow Slovaks did not allay my apprehension. I was returning to my homeland which, for me, was still enemy territory. Regardless, the night before we left, Mato and I secretly agreed that once we crossed into Slovakia, we'd never return to the camp. We'd help each other to reach the Russian lines. We also agreed not to tell the other three until we reached Bratislava. As important to the success of our mission as Bednarik was because of his connection to Sano Mach, the less he knew the better. He was strongly patriotic and supported Slovakia's causes without question. Mato and I couldn't be sure about the other two, so why take chances?

The ride to Vienna took all day and all night. We agreed to bypass Vienna. We arrived mid-morning and, without stopping for a thing, took a tram from West Bahnhof to East Bahnhof where we boarded the train for Bratislava. Our decision not to stop in Vienna, go straight to Bratislava and then try for home, would in no way affect our mission. We wouldn't let down our comrades in the camp. We'd see the Interior Minister to request the supplies before going our separate ways.

At the Austrian border, the border guards checked our passports, saw our document from Messerschmitt and quickly let us through. Slovak border guards did the same.

We reached Bratislava mid-afternoon. It was dreary and cold. Our worn out clothes provided no insulation against the wintry conditions, nor did my skin-and-bones. I was down to a hundred pounds.

We were staying at the Y.M.C.A. On the way, within minutes of my arrival, the one thing I had feared most happened. We passed a couple from Presov. I recognized them at once. They had been our neighbors in the building at 65 Hlinkova Street next to ours at 67 Hlinkova. Though I had a beard, I knew they also recognized me. They stopped but I kept walking. I was badly shaken.

It was only a matter of half an hour between the time I saw the couple and the time we reached our room but I was already feverish and sick from fear. Conditions at the Y didn't help. It was rundown. Our room was more squalid than the barracks. Undoubtedly, the lice felt at home. More unsettling than the filth were some blood stains splattered on the walls.

The next day I felt no better. I told the group to go on without me. Had I been better, I was still too frightened to go into the street, let alone walk through the Interior Ministry and stand before the country's second most important person, Sano Mach. Mach, a rabid anti-Semite, was also eminently corruptible. He had introduced the yellow star exemption in 1942 to line the government's coffers and his own pockets. (He was tried after the war and hanged, along with his President, Monsignor Tiso.) Mato assured the others they could handle the mission without me, heading off any pressure that I accompany them.

They returned late that afternoon. The report was favorable. They had seen the Interior Minister, told him of the Slovaks' plight in the camp and explained their mission. The Minister was furious about his countrymen's predicament. He promised to arrange for food, blankets, and clothing to be sent to the camp as soon as the paperwork was completed. He ordered us to remain in Slovakia and not return to Augsburg at all. He said he had the right to countermand our orders because we were taken illegally in the first place.

I have no idea whether the supplies were shipped or, if they were, whether they reached Augsburg. None of us was ready to stay in Bratislava to find out.

Travel in Slovakia required a permit. Our permit was valid only as far as Zilina. I had Treuer add Zilina to our order pleading that if I had the chance during our mission, I'd like to visit friends there. Travel permits were available in Bratislava but I was afraid of going into public to obtain one. I told Bednarik and Mato, who were coming to Zilina with me, that I had a friend, Jan Pavlovcin, living in Bytca fifteen miles northwest of Zilina. We could stop there to obtain our permits. They agreed, Mato knowing the real reason for my suggestion. Next day, Longauer and Potacok said their goodbyes and headed home east. Bednarik, Mato, and I, headed north on the first leg of our journeys home.

Chapter 11

Crossing

On the train to Bytca, my heart should have been bursting with joy. I was going home. Instead, I suffered a new despair. I had lived through six and a half years of terror, the past five months in an abyss. The future was rarely something I dared think about, let alone a future worth living. In those brief moments when I mustered enough hope to believe I might endure, the dream of home buttressed that hope. Home was the reason to live, the reason for living. With the dream so close to coming true I feared the reality. Did I still have a home? Were Herman and his family alive? Had Maria survived? To have gone through so much, to have come so far, to at last be so close to the exquisite moment of passing through the threshold of my brother's apartment, only to walk into an empty room, back to nothing, to no one, would break me. My parents and two brothers were in America, true, but they were in another universe. Heading toward Bytca I came to understand there was another dimension to despair.

It took almost an entire day to make the 100 mile trip from Bratislava to Bytca. Inside, the train was packed with forlorn civilians and a few, begrimed Slovak soldiers; the Slovak army was now a remnant. Outside, the only cheering sights were the retreating German Army and the greening just beginning to show through the winter-dead meadows. When we arrived, I told Mato and Bednarik to wait for me while I saw my friend.

Jan Pavlovcin, his wife and two children, lived with his in-laws. The house was roomy enough for two people, for six it was cramped. I was warmed by his effusive greeting. He had grown up with Herman in Dlhe and they continued their friendship in Presov where Pavlovcin was our company's banker. His excitement moderated when I explained why I had come. Though the war was almost over, we were in what remained of Axis-held Slovakia where a Jew was still in mortal danger as were those caught hiding one.

Pavlovcin offered me a welcome bowl of hot soup and bread. My presence obviously made him uncomfortable so I ate hurriedly. There was little time to catch up on events. He had left Presov several months before to get his family out of the war zone. At that time, the city was a German armed camp. Civilians were encouraged to leave. Not only were they in the way, the Germans needed their homes for billeting. The Germans were also wary of civilians helping the Russians. Pavlovcin said the war was winding down. It was only a matter of months, maybe weeks, before it was over. The Allies had almost completely overrun Germany. Russians lines were about fifty miles east of Bytca, just over the Lower Tatra mountains. He hadn't heard a thing from or about my brother or my wife. I told Pavlovcin a little about my odyssey, not wanting to overstay my welcome. Even with only a brief summary, he was visibly shaken by what I had been through.

Pavlovcin arranged for Mato, Bednarik, and I to stay at the Y.M.C.A., a dilapidated one-story building with a dozen cramped rooms. The next day he took us to the Notary Public which, unlike Notaries in the United States, was an official government agency. Pavlovcin had a high-placed connection who was so impressed by our mission for Messerschmitt and our documents emblazoned with the Messerschmitt seal that he saluted us with a "Na Straz," (On Guard) and promptly issued us travel permits. The permits were good for six days, from 31 March 1945-the following day-to 6 April 1945. They authorized travel from Bytca to Korytnica, about forty miles southeast. According to Bednarik, Korytnica was the village closest to a good crossing point he knew over the Lower Tatra mountains. His village, already in Russian hands, was just beyond the eastern side. Korytnica had no train station so we bought tickets to Helpa, a small town ten miles from Korytnica. The next day, after a relieved Jan Pavlovcin wished us well, we were on our way.

We arrived mid-afternoon. The walk from Helpa to Korytnica was slow. When German soldiers weren't stopping us to ask for our papers, they were forcing us off the road to make way for their retreating men and materiel. When we were stopped it was with disinterest, more from habit than from a concern for security. The soldiers looked at our papers indifferently, saw the Messerschmitt authorization and let us pass without question or comment.

We passed through a few small villages, stopping in each to beg for food. We had been away from the camp seven days, still we hadn't had enough to eat to take the slightest edge off our hunger. Hunger had become a permanent affliction.

Displaced people were wandering everywhere. The farmers were sympathetic and helpful to their suffering countrymen. It was near Easter. The spirit of the season inclined them to share what they could: a piece of bread, soup, a potato.

By nightfall we were still a few miles from Korytnica. A farmer let us sleep in his barn. We chipped in some of the little money we had left from the three thousand crowns Oberleutnant Treuer had given us for a bottle of liquor. It was generally believed that liquor gave you energy. We knew we'd need all the energy we could summon from our weakened bodies for the climb the next day. Before turning in we took more than a few sips from the bottle for practice. Though I had never been a drinker, the liquor felt good in my empty stomach. It also took the chill from my bones.

The three of us had spoken little since leaving Bratislava. The drinking made us more passive. We had no spirit or pep. We moved like machines. Misery had turned us into zombies. Not even the prospect of going home alleviated our weariness.

Late the next morning we reached Korytnica and the foothills of the Lower Tatra mountains. After begging a breakfast of soup and bread, we took fortifying sips from our bottle and began the climb. It was fifteen miles up, across and down to the foothills of the eastern slope. Under favorable conditions it would have taken less than a day. It took us two days. The climb, though arduous and slow, was steady. There was little snow. We believed the liquor was helping our progress. But Bednarik warned that when we neared the summit and on the descent, snow would become a factor. The eastern slope took longer to thaw each spring than the western slope.

We reached the snow line near the summit before dusk. Exhausted and starving we camped for the night. We broke branches from a pine tree and made crude bedding to keep off the frozen ground. We ate the last of the bread and potatoes we had saved and huddled together for warmth in the frigid night air.

At daybreak we started our trek again. The snow got deeper. We came within a few yards of a mother and child frozen solid in upright walking positions, like statues, but didn't have the energy to walk over to them. We reached the summit and began our descent. The snow was waist deep. Going downhill was harder than the climb. Each step required effort-lifting one leg, pushing it through the snow, sinking into the snow, lifting the other leg to push on another step. I had it easiest. I was third in line, following Bednarik and Mato. I was walking in their pathway. Still, the little stamina I had was giving out. We stopped from time to time to take a sip of liquor to buoy our energy, if not our spirits. As the going became increasingly arduous, our "energy breaks" became more frequent until we had to ration sips.

I tried distracting my thoughts from the ordeal. I gave myself a silent pep talk, "Hold out a while longer. You're only a few miles from the Russians and freedom. Freedom! Then it's home." The thought of home again aroused the despair that no one would be there. I tried to fight my anxiety by forcing myself to think positively. I had endured being a fugitive, capture, beating, imprisonment, discovery. I had been among the beasts and survived. I was so close... My feet stuck in the snow. Then I collapsed.

Practically unconscious, I half-heartedly tried to cry out but couldn't. Or didn't want to. I was lying flat on my back but felt as if I were levitating in a suspended state of bliss. A feeling of warmth came over me. I felt a peace and tranquility I had never known. I saw a beautiful, lush, green valley. An eden. My hunger vanished. I felt no pain. I was weightless. I felt wonderful!

Suddenly Mato was shaking me, shouting at me to get up. I lay there not wanting to move. I told him to leave me alone for a while. They should go on. I'd follow later. I had to rest. Mato kept shouting that I had to get up and keep walking otherwise I'd freeze to death. He and Bednarik took me by either arm and jerked me to my feet. They put me in the middle, closed the distance between us to a few feet and, without another word, plowed on. I followed, moving like a robot.

I don't know how much time passed or the distance we travelled before my first awareness of anything since the collapse. The snow was disappearing. The going was easier. A few hours later we reached the base of the Lower Tatra's eastern slope. It was dark. All we could see were a few primitive huts about a quarter of a mile apart. I thought only about food and rest. I was too spent to celebrate being on free soil; to enjoy the relief from no longer having to fear being a Jew; to rejoice in the triumph of survival.

We stopped at the first hut we came to. I had all I could do to keep from collapsing in front of the surprised farmer. After Mato briefly told him our story, the farmer treated us like heroes. He gave us our first decent meal in months: hot soup, bread, baked potatoes, and hot cabbage. He offered us a small unheated shed for the night. After years of living as a sub-human in deprivation and dread, at the mercy of malevolent authority and fate, I fell asleep before I could savor my first night as a free man.

The next morning we prepared to go thinking we could travel freely now that we were in Russian-held territory. The farmer informed us that the Russians were no less bureaucratic than any other people. We would need travel permits. He didn't know where to obtain them and suggested we try a Russian command post a few miles away. He cautioned us to be careful how we dealt with the Russians, they were somewhat backward. A friend had told him that a few days ago in a nearby town, a Russian soldier wearing a large alarm clock around his neck asked for the time. Apparently, the clock was the first the Russian had ever seen. When his friend looked at his wristwatch the Russian was amazed. He had never seen a wristwatch before, either. The Russian demanded the friend take him to a watchmaker where the Russian ordered him to make four small watches, like the one on the friend's wrist, from the large alarm clock and to keep whatever was left over in payment. It was the first laugh I had in a long time.

After the war, I learned that some Russian soldiers had not seen many modern conveniences, such as an indoor toilet. They used the water in the bowl to wash themselves. The sardines they were used to eating came in the form of a paste. When they came across toothpaste, they smeared it on bread and ate it. They pillaged everything new that they saw. Slovak farmers may have been primitive but compared to the Russians they were urbane.

Soon after we reported to the Russian command post we knew we had made a mistake. The commander thought he had caught three German spies. We repeated our story over and over trying to convince him that he was in error. It was no use. He had us detained and thrown into a shed that served as a makeshift jail. Sitting with my companions, I thought, "Here we go again. To have gone through all we had only to wind up prisoners again." I remembered what Oberleutnant Treuer told me before we left on our mission. That Germans soldiers on the front lines had orders not to take Russian prisoners because of the Wehrmacht's food shortage. I considered what that would mean in retribution to a German or German sympathizer caught by the Russians.

The Russian commander interrogated us individually. When it was my turn, he repeated what he had told the others. Our story was too fantastic. He knew something about what the Germans had done in the concentration camps. For us to have survived, let alone have been entrusted with a mission as non-German representatives of Messerschmitt, was too outrageous to believe. "No," he judged, "you are German spies." In desperation I said, "How could I be a German spy, I am a Jew. My name is Jozef Kornfeld. I live in Presov." Instead of helping my cause, my admission made him all the more skeptical. A Jew surviving a concentration camp? "No," he repeated, "you are a German spy."

I cried, "So help me God, I'm telling you the truth!"

He grabbed his pistol and shook it in my face shouting, "God? The only person who can help you is me. You see this?" He pointed the gun at me. "If I want to, you can be dead right now. Never mind God, only I can help you." As a Communist his atheism was so ingrained that the mere mention of God was a serious affront to his Marxist-Leninist beliefs.

In desperation, I told the Russian commander that he could verify my identity by contacting Captain Kubik of the Czechoslovakian Brigade. The Czechoslovakian Brigade fought side-by-side with the Russian army against the Germans. I explained that I was in the lumber business in Presov and Kubik's father was a lumber broker we did business with, which is how I knew the son. I told the commander that I also knew that Captain Kubik became a partisan leader fighting for the Russians before he joined the Czechoslovakian Brigade. The Russian commander scratched his chin and dismissed me with a wave of the hand.

I was returned to the shed under guard. Outside a few soldiers were cooking a breakfast of borscht, a concoction of rolled dough made from wheat tossed into boiling water that turned into a black, lumpy soup. They offered us a bowl. It was warm and filled our bellies, but it tasted worse than anything the Germans had ever given us.

We paced the rest of the day in apprehension. Sleep that night was fitful, beset by familiar problems:

hunger, lice, and fear for our lives.

A day later the Russian commander summoned us. Without another word he said, perfunctorily, we could go. To this day I don't know what changed his mind, whether he contacted Kubik or had checked on Mato and Bednarik who lived in the region.

Hardly able to contain our relief, we hurried out of the camp and almost ran the few miles to the nearest town to obtain Russian travel permits. The permits were bilingual-in Slovak and Russian. The issuing agency was part of the new National Council which had replaced all Slovak agencies. Only citizens the Russians absolutely believed to be anti-German were given jobs in the Council.

In a matter of hours I held a new permit, valid until 30 April 1945, authorizing Ludovit Argay to travel to Presov. It was April 9th. I was about 35 miles from Banska Bystrica, from where I had run for my life what seemed like an eon ago. I had seventeen days to cover the roughly hundred miles to Presov. Officially, I was almost Jozef Kornfeld again. I was almost home.

A day later the kind camp commander's [illegible] without another word he said, permission: we could go [illegible] day. I don't know what changed his mind, whether he had [illegible] one between Nato and [illegible] lived in the [illegible].

Hardly [illegible] our [illegible] we hurried out of the camp and almost [illegible] two miles to the nearest station to obtain [illegible] new permits. The [illegible] were [illegible] and [illegible]. The issuing agency was part of the new [illegible] which had replaced all Slovak agencies. [illegible] absolutely believe [illegible] were [illegible] in the Council.

Chapter 12

Home

It was an emotional goodbye. Bednarik, Mato, and I clasped hands and hugged, wishing each other good luck. For Mato and me, parting was especially touching. We made impassioned pledges to remain friends and meet after the war. We did correspond for a year but lost touch. Alas, we never did meet again. I have never forgotten Mato Luptak and think of him often with affection and gratitude. By keeping my secret he saved my life. It was a brave and noble act in a time when human life was cheap and a Jew's life was worthless, except to an informer. Turning me in would have meant reward for Mato, improving his lot when he, like the rest of us, was so hungry and miserable.

We went our separate ways looking like gypsies. Bednarik headed south to Lubietova, the village where I spent the first night of my capture. Mato headed south to Banska Bystrica. I went east, a hungry, lice-ridden, one hundred pound skeleton. Yet, I walked straight, my steps lively, my pace brisk. I was free! And except for my anxiety about what I'd find in Presov, I was without dread. Until you lose your freedom, until you live endless days in the relentless fear that each one may be your last, there is no way to describe the relief, the almost unbearable lightness of being that comes with liberation. I had my life back. I was reborn. The time of terror was over. It was overwhelming.

I don't know how long I walked, my euphoria a narcotic, before exhaustion brought me back to the reality of my immediate needs. I sat by the side of the pitted, dirt road to rest. With growing concern, I wondered how I would make the one hundred miles to Presov.

The countryside teemed with activity. Thousands of refugees-men, women, and children-headed in every direction except due west where the Germans still held out. Russian and Czech military trucks passed back and forth packed with those lucky enough to have hitch-hiked a ride. I lifted myself up and stood at the edge of the road, thumb pointing east.

Some rides lasted only a few miles, others took me from one village to another. On foot, I begged for food, never coming up empty. Farmers everywhere, despite their circumstances, had great empathy for their displaced countrymen. A few villages even set up outdoor kitchens with produce available until dark. At night, if I couldn't find a shack, with winter losing its grip I was able to sleep outside without much discomfort. When I came to a town that had train service anywhere east, I got on board and took it as far as it went. With so many roadbeds and railroad bridges destroyed, there was no direct train service anywhere for long distances. The trains, like the trucks, were packed. If you had money you paid for your ticket and rode inside a passenger car. If you had no money, the trainmen let you ride free on top of the train or in the open box cars. At the end of the line I started walking and hitch-hiking again. The further east I went, away from the front, the fewer Russians vehicles there were. I hitched rides from farmers and townspeople in their hay wagons and buggies.

I was by myself but not alone. Wherever I went

there was an esprit among the refugees. We had much in common: a shared national heritage, hunger, and suffering. War had driven most of them from their homes, dispersed their families, and destroyed loved ones and friends. Conversation was compassionate but not overly inquiring. Where are you from? Where did you end up? Where are you going? People had been through enough, they didn't want to hear any more about travail. I avoided mentioning that I was a Jew. Who knew what anti-Semitic resentments existed among the refugees. Even had I not been afraid to say I was a Jew, I still would have been reluctant to do so. Living as a second-class citizen for so long, my feeling of inferiority was ingrained.

The closer to Presov I got, the more apprehensive I grew about whether Herman, Alice, their children, and Maria would be there. I wondered what had happened to my sister Esther and her family, whom I still saw calling out from behind the barred windows of the boxcar in Margecany that horrendous day three years ago. I thought about my friends, David Sekely, Alice Roth, Sessi, Susan, Fritz, George, Saul, Edith, Monica.

Aggressively, I pursued any transportation that speeded my journey. When I wasn't riding, I walked as fast as I could, resting only when exhaustion compelled it. Freedom was intoxicating. There'd be a future after all, something to look forward to, even more so if my family were alive. I was still hungry. The lice were still biting; after so long I though of them as companions. I was as skinny as a dried-out herring and probably smelled as bad. But now that I was free, the lice and the hunger were tolerable. Freedom had given me strength. For the first time in so long, I indulged myself in musings of how sweet life used to be and would be again. For the first time in so long, I could dream.

Four days after I had started the final leg of my

journey from near Banska Bystrica, I reached Kysak where I was lucky enough to catch a train to Presov. In Kysak, I smiled remembering the stunning Hungarian aristocrat who taught me about being a "gentleman," and Frau Kesselbauer, and Nula.

A few hours later, the train entered the suburbs of the city. I was so inured to destruction that seeing familiar buildings and neighborhoods in rubble had little effect on me. What did strike me was the welling of familiar apprehensions. Although the Russians had long since liberated Presov and the Slovak government no longer held sway, I couldn't shake the feeling that I was back in the same environment where I had lived in such wrenching fear for so long. On the streets I saw familiar faces that reminded me of the people who had persecuted me. I almost felt like a fugitive again. I couldn't disconnect the baggage of memory. It weighed down my feeling of freedom.

I half ran the familiar two miles to my brother's apartment. Someone else was living there. My apprehension approached panic. I headed for 67 Hlinkova Street. Heart thumping, I walked through the courtyard, entered the building, and stepped into the hallway that led to the office of Malik and Company. It was all so familiar, yet, it was as if I were seeing it for the first time.

No one was around. A spectral emptiness pervaded the place. Slowly, I opened the office door. At a small table, in the middle of the sparsely furnished room that had been converted into cramped living quarters, sat Herman, Alice, Hedy, and Paul. It looked as if they had been waiting for me.

Hedy was the first to spot me, shouting, "Uncle Joe!" The others screamed, jumped up and, as one, ran to me, tears streaming down their faces. The years of discrimination, persecution, deprivation, fear, terror, and hunger, had done something to me. Here was the moment I had dreamed about, the moment that helped sustain me. My family had survived! Here they were hugging and kissing me. Instead of deep joy, overwhelming happiness, inexpressible relief, I had no emotion. It felt as if I wasn't really there, but only observing the scene at a distance, as a spectator. I felt detached. I had dried up. Becoming human again would take time.

Alice held me at arm's length, gave me the once over, and declared that I was too skinny, I must eat before we did another thing. Despite the hunger that had been so relentless, I was too spent to eat. Alice insisted. As I slowly put the morsels into my mouth, not aware of what I was eating, we sat in silence staring at one another. Alice said, almost as if to herself, "Jozef, look at you, what you must have been through." Then their questions came.

They listened to my tale in shock and disbelief. The more I revealed, the more they treated me as one who had truly come back from the dead. They couldn't get enough. After I told them of my odyssey for the second time, they just shook their heads and stared. I used the silence to break off my story and find out about them.

They had spent their entire time in hiding with the farmer who had dug the pit for them under his pig sty. Every day for four months in the dark, damp hole, they unsuccessfully dodged pig waste. Every night they climbed out of the pit, washed as best they could in the bitter cold, ate, and slept. Each morning they crawled back into the pit for another day. The Russians liberated their area in February. It took them two weeks to reach Presov. With their apartment occupied, they turned the company office into home. There was no work, much of Presov was in ruins. There was a shortage of everything. For a time, they lived on the little savings they had left. When the bank opened, because his credit had been so good, Herman borrowed more money. But money wasn't as valuable as goods and services. Barter was the main means of subsistence. Herman had only his good will to barter. Daily, he bicycled to a farmer friend who had once worked for him hauling logs and brought home potatoes, vegetables, and sometimes a chicken. He had always treated the farmers well. With his family in such desperate need, they were happy to return the favor. Starting the business had to wait until people put their lives back together and had needs beyond food, shelter, and clothing.

As much as I wanted to hear more, my level of fatigue became unbearable. I couldn't stay awake any longer. Alice put a mattress in the old conference room. I slept the sleep of the dead.

I don't know how much later it was when through my sedated state I heard screaming and Hedy's voice shouting, "Uncle Joe's home. Uncle Joe's home." The door to the conference room opened and there stood Maria. I couldn't speak. I just laid there. She bent down and we covered each other with hugs and kisses. She had been living in the office with Herman and his family since her return in March. That afternoon she had been out looking for supplies and trying to barter her seamstress skills for food.

Somewhat refreshed from my nap, we sat around the table drinking in one another's presence. They insisted that I retell my story to Maria. But I wanted to hear what had happened to her first.

She had stayed on the farm where she had gone into hiding until the uprising at Banska Bystrica. Then she fled to the newly liberated area. She found another farmer who took her in until the Russians came. She returned to Presov in March, located Herman and they had been living in the office since.

Six "dead" people had been reunited. We were all thinner, harder, and older-looking, even the children. But we were alive and together!

We stayed up most of the night telling and retelling our stories of survival and "feasting" on the little Alice had in the cupboard. No one cared that we were eating the next day's rations. Once again, overcome with fatigue, I settled down on the mattress in the conference room. On that glorious night, the most luxuriant bed of down couldn't have been more comfortable.

The next day I began the struggle to pick up the pieces of my life and return to it some semblance of routine and normalcy. It was not to be. Despite my ordeal, I had a military obligation to fulfill. It was the law that all able-bodied men, ages eighteen to fifty-five, had to report for induction within forty-eight hours of their return from wherever. I told the authorities what I'd been through. They said the war was still on. It was my patriotic duty to serve.

As the Russians liberated an area of Slovakia, it ceased to exist as a Slovak political entity. It became part of the new Republic of Czechoslovakia whose Czechoslovakian Brigade still needed men to fight alongside the Russians.

The military authorities appraised my emaciated condition and considered themselves generous by giving me a two week deferment before I had to report to the army camp at Levoca, forty miles west of Presov. I had only fourteen days to fatten up and regain my strength before I had to begin walking and hitch-hiking again; trains between Presov and Levoca were not running.

During those two weeks I tried adjusting to my new old life. I did what I could to help Alice around the room that served as home. I went on errands for my brother and Maria if they weren't too fatiguing.

The day I left for duty was rending. After being apart for so long and suffering so greatly, after being together so briefly, I was being separated from my family again. It was almost more than I could bear. Everyone reassured me that it was only for a few months and I'd be only forty miles away. But I needed to be home with my family. I needed emotional nourishment just as much as I required nourishment from food. What I didn't need was to be back in a barracks with a sergeant shouting and ordering me about. What I didn't need was military discipline and the physical rigors of military life.

It took me two days to reach the camp at Levoca. No sooner had I arrived when I was told I could go home. The war was over! If I were needed in the future, they would call me. The trip back to Presov also took two days but relief and happiness made it seem much shorter.

I was home to stay. Spring was in full bloom. The future I never dared believe I'd live to see was before me.

Afterword

In the summer of 1945 Jozef Kornfeld changed his last name to Kalina, a common Slovak surname. He wanted to disassociate himself from its German derivation. He wanted nothing to do with anything German. Nor did he wish to carry a name that had drawn to him so much unwelcome attention.

In the few months since returning to Presov from his Holocaust odyssey, when an acquaintance recognized him in the street and called, Kornfeld; when he reported for military duty as "Kornfeld;" when he went to government offices on business and the clerk called out, "Kornfeld;" when he saw, "Kornfeld," on company documents he had processed during the time of terror; the fear and threat he had endured for so long jolted him again. The war was over but Jozef Kornfeld's wounds were still open and raw. The change of name would help him to begin a new identity in a new life.

Joseph Kalina remained in Czechoslovakia until the Communists came to power in 1948. He emigrated to Canada and then to the United States in 1955. He and Maria were divorced in 1947. Herman and his family emigrated to Israel in 1948.

Since retiring from his lumber business, Joseph Kalina speaks regularly to high school and college students about his odyssey and the lessons of discrimination to be learned from the Holocaust. His philosophy has been tempered by his experience. He speaks as a realist believing in only what is visible and tangible.

For his efforts in behalf of Holocaust survivors, Kalina was named by Governor Mario Cuomo to the New York State Holocaust Memorial Commission; the New York State Assembly passed a Legislative Resolution in 1991 honoring Kalina's work as a Holocaust historian; and he was the 1990 recipient of the prestigious Yavner Award, presented by the Regents of the University of the State of New York.

Jozef's graduation picture from forestry
school in Humenne - 1936

Some members of Jozef's clique at one of their Sunday get togethers. (Left to right) George, Suzan, Mitzi, Jozef, Maria, Lily. Only Jozef and Maria survived.

Jozef and Maria - 1940

Esther, her husband Eli, and their two children - 1936. Standing is brother David who emigrated to America shortly after this picture was taken. As a soldier in the U.S. Army, he fought the Germans in Italy.

In the woods with a timber-loading crew - 1937.
(Jozef is standing rear center)

Herman (front) and Jozef (rear center) with Gendarmes at the burned down saw mill in Svidnik - 1943

Ludovit Argay – 1985

Picture of the Virgin Mary given to Jozef
by Ludovit Argay's mother for good luck.

Jozef's nephew and niece, Paul and Hedy - 1946

Alice and Herman (seated) with Jozef's niece, Martha – 1972

Train ticket [In German and Slovak].

German Slovak Transportation	Day of Purchase	Return trip ends
	23.03.1945	5.22.45

Travel ticket 3 class for one adult on express train
Workers return ticket
from: Augsburg Main Station
to: Bratislava
via: Munich, Vienna....
and return 59.05 RM

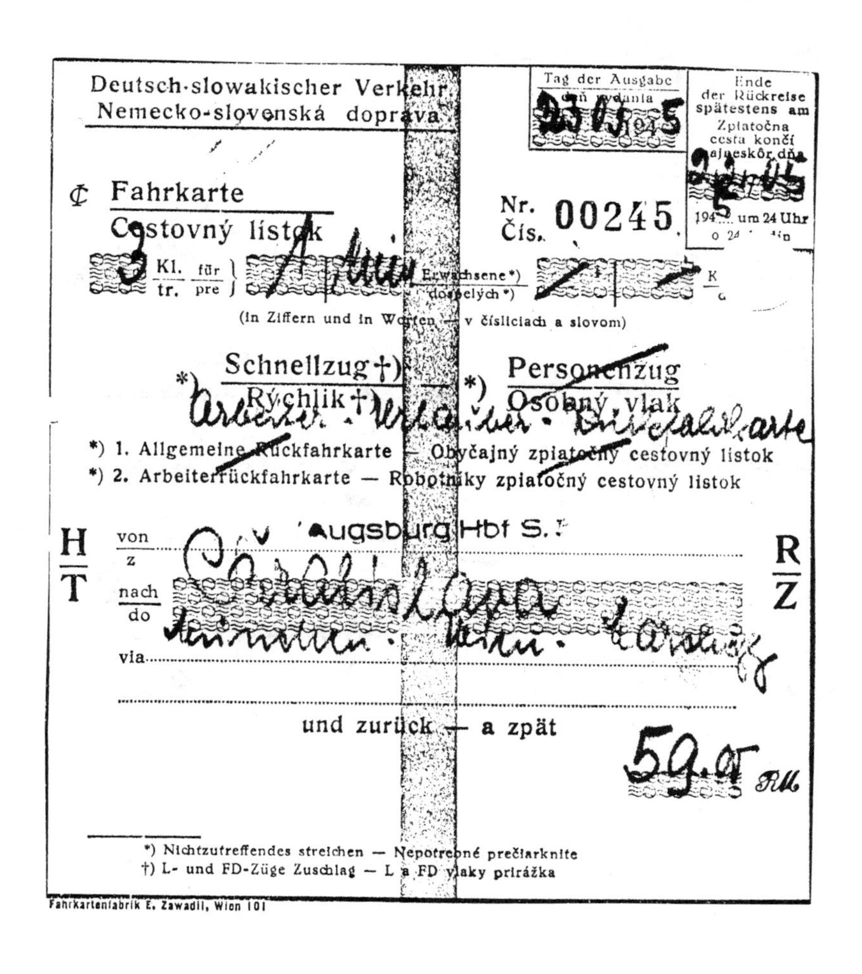
Deutsch-slowakischer Verkehr
Nemecko-slovenská doprava

Tag der Ausgabe
dňa vydania
23.03.1945

Ende der Rückreise spätestens am
Zpiatočna cesta končí najneskôr dňa
194_ um 24 Uhr
o 24 hodin

Fahrkarte
Cestovný lístok

Nr.
Čís. 00245

3 Kl. für / tr. pre 1 Adult Erwachsene*) / dospelých*)

(In Ziffern und in Worten — v číslicach a slovom)

*) Schnellzug †) / Rýchlik †) — *) ~~Personenzug~~ / Osobný vlak

*) 1. Allgemeine Rückfahrkarte — Obyčajný zpiatočný cestovný lístok
*) 2. Arbeiterrückfahrkarte — Robotníky zpiatočný cestovný lístok

H/T von / z Augsburg Hbf S.
nach / do Bratislava
via .... R/Z

und zurück — a zpät

59.05 RM

*) Nichtzutreffendes streichen — Nepotrebné prečiarknite
†) L- und FD-Züge Zuschlag — L a FD vlaky prirážka

Fahrkartenfabrik E. Zawadil, Wien 101

Travel permit issued by the Russian authorities for travel from Banska Bystrica to Presov [in Slovak and Russian].

National Commission in Banska Bystrica

Travel Permit
Citizen: Ludovit Argay
profession: Wood manipulator
born: 23.VIII.1917
resides: Presov
is allowed to travel from B. Bystrica to
......Presov.............
in official capacity
Permit is valid to 30.IV.1945

Národný výbor
v Banskej Bystrici.

Evid. č. 1288/45.
V Banskej Bystrici dňa 9.IV. 1945.

CESTOVNÉ POVOLENIE.

Občan /:ka:/ Ludovit Argay....
zamestnaním manipulant drevom
nar. dňa 23.VIII.1917 v Hatalov
bytom v ....Prešov...................
môže cestovať z B. Bystrice do ...
....Prešov.................. a späť
v záležitosti ....služobnej.....
Povolenie platí do 30.IV....1945.

predseda: tajomník:

ПУТЕВОЙ ПРОПУСК

граж. Людевит Аргай
занятие манипулянт
рожден 23.VIII.1917 г. Гаталов
жительством Прешов
может ездить из Б. Быстрице
до Прешов а назад
по делам служебным
Разрешение действ. 30.IV.45.

Change of name decree.

Number: 4015/IV-1945 date 5.June 1945
Subject: Jozef Kornfeld, Kosice,
change of name

<u>Decree</u>

According to-U8 law No. 31/1942 Sl.z. I fulfill the request of Jozef Kornfeld, born 12.march.1917 in Dlhe over Cirocha district Snina, belonging there too I permit to change the name to Kalina.

This change applies to his wife Maria, born Markovic 12.may 1922 in Trevisov.

Of this is notified: Josef Kornfeld in Kosice to present a copy of this decree with a request to the state matriculate office to note this change in the matriculate records.

Assistant official:
[Signature]

POVERENÍCTVO SNR PRE VECI VNÚTORNÉ
EXPOZITÚRA V KOŠICIACH

Číslo: 4015/IV-1945. V Košiciach dňa 5.júna 1945.
Predmet: Jozef Kornfeld, Košice,
zmena priezviska.

<u>V ý m e r .</u>

Na základe §-u 8 zák.čís.31/1942 Sl.z. vyhovujem žiadosti Jozefa Kornfelda, narodeného dňa 12.marca 1917 v Dlhom nad Cirochou, okres Snina, príslušného tamtiež a povoľujem zmenu jeho priezviska na " K A L I N A ".

Táto zmena vzťahuje sa aj na jeho manželku rod. Máriu Markovičovú, nar. 12.mája 1922 v Trebišove.

O tom sa upovedomuje:

Jozef Kornfeld v Košiciach s tým, aby jeden exemplár tohoto výmeru predložil so žiadosťou na príslušný štátny matričný úrad cieľom opravenia matričného záznamu.

Zástupca povereníka:
[signature]

6 Tage

Reichskarte für Urlauber

Gültig im deutschen Reichsgebiet — 5. Ausgabe

Diese Karte enthält Einzelabschnitte über insgesamt:
1910 g Brot, davon
1350 g R-Brot
200 g Fleisch
130 g Butter
60 g Margarine
150 g Marmelade
200 g Zucker
125 g Nährmittel
50 g Kaffee-Ersatz
60 g Käse

Ausgabestelle EA:

Name: ....

Wohnort: ....

Straße: ....

Ohne Namenseintragung ungültig! Nicht übertragbar! Sorgfältig aufbewahren! — Abtrennen der Einzelabschnitte nur durch Kleinverteiler, Gaststätten usw.

Ration stamps for the mission to Bratislava

Travel permit issued in Velk-a Bytca [In Slovak and German].

Notary office in V. Bytca
Date 10/1640/1945

One way Permit to Travel

Name: Argay Ludovit,
Born: 23 August 1917 in the village of Hatalov,
Occupation: Worker
Residence: Augsburg at the present time. V. Bytca

is permitted one way travel by train
from V. Bytca to Korytnica
and return from 31 march 1945 to 6 april 1945

It is valid only upon presentation of a valid I.D. and a stamped travel ticket.

Notársky úrad v [redacted] V.Bytči . **Notariatsamt in** Veľk-á Bytča -
Číslo - Zahl: 10/1640/1945. Dátum 30.marca 1945.

Jednorazové povolenie na cestovanie.
Einmalige Reisebewilligung.

Meno - Name: A r g a y Ľudovit,
narodený dňa - geboren am: 23.augusta 1917 v obci Hatalov,
zamestnanie - Beruf: robotník,
bydlisko - Wohnung: Ausburg - t.č.V.Bytča

povoľuje sa **jednorazové** cestovanie vlakom - wird die einmalige Reise

z - aus: [redacted] V.Bytča do - nach: Korytnica

a zpäť v čase od 31.marca 1945 do 6.apríla 1945
u. zurück in der Zeit vom bis bewilligt.

Platí iba pri súčasnom predložení preukazu osobnej totožnosti a po orazítkovaní výdajňou cestovných lístkov.
Ist nur in Verbindung mit einem Personalausweis und nach erfolgter Abstempelung durch die Fahrkartenausgabe giltig.

Exemption from wearing the Jewish star.

<u>Police headquarters in Presov</u>

No:....3782....../1942 USBO Presov, date 5 June 1942

Subject: <u>Jozef Kornfeld</u>
a Presov resident - freed of carrying the Jewish marking.

Certificate.

The Police headquarters of Presov according 3 on the announcement of the Interior Ministry of March 2, 1942 Number 103 hereby confirms, that Jew Jozef Kornfeld, residing in Presov, Slovenska 56 is according point D/2 of the mentioned ordinance freed from the obligation of wearing a Jewish marking.

This permit is valid to 31 July 1942./two/.

On guard!
Gov. advisor and chief of police

Policajné riaditeľstvo v Prešove.

Číslo:...3782....../1942 ÚŠBO. Prešov, dňa 5. júna 1942....

Predmet: Jozef K o r n f e l d-
prešovský obyvateľ-oslobodený
od nosenia židovského označenia.

O s v e d č e n i e .

Policajné riaditeľstvo v Prešove na základe § 3.vyhlášky minis vnútra zo dňa 2.marca 1942,číslo 103 týmto úradne potvrdzuje,že Žid-
........Jozef K o r n f e l d,...............bytom v Prešove.......
..Slovenská 56........ulica čís...56......je podľa bodu...d./...§ 2.citovano vyhlášky oslobodený-á od povinnosti nosiť židovské označenie.

Osvedčenie je platné do..31.júla 1942./dva/................

Na stráž!

Vládny radca a policajný riaditeľ

Employment permit (front).

THE MINISTRY OF INTERIOR

Number 5709 I/25-1941 Bratislava the day of 9.XI.1941

Subject: Lignum Company
in Presov.
request for a permit to employ a
Jew Jozef Kornfeld

DECREE

According to the announcement of the chairman of the central economy office of the 28th of October 1941 number Prez. 4.401/1941 published in the official publication under the number 492 and according 43 sec. 3 nat. no. 198/1941 Slovak law.

I permit

petitioner Lignum lumber
to employ the Jew Jozef Kornfeld
born 12.III.1917 residing in Kapisova
under the following conditions:

1. The named Jew is allowed to be employed only as a forest coordinator and only for the above named company in the work place of Presov.

2. Remuneration and compensation for this employee is established as of 1. October 1941:

   a) salary monthly 900 Ks [Crowns]

   b) no other benefits

3. This permit is valid to 31. December 1941 and can be removed by the Inner Ministry at any time.

4. The employer is obligated to inform the Inner Ministry, through the appropriate local district, or (state police) office, any change in the service (or work) order with the employed Jew.

5. The employer and the employed Jew are obliged to find a substitute non Jew worker to train in the same field and skill for which the employer is asking to employ a Jew.

This permit is not transferable to any other person and can not be substituted (consent) by any other office to fill the requirement to employ the above mentioned Jew, even according other rules.

To violate the conditions of this permit is punishable according 48 nar. no. 198/1941 Sl. law with a financial fine of 1000 Ks to 100.000 Ks or jail from 10 days to 60 days.

The remuneration for this official act I assess according to policy 4, section B escalating scale of the government rule No. 360/1940 Sl. law in the sum of 100 Ks payable upon presentation under consequences of execution plus 6% interest from the due day.

For this permission I also assess for the benefit of a fund established to maintain the work camps of Jews a special levy of 2400 Ks payable to the Slovak Hypotace Bank under account number 4.800

There is no appeal against this decree.

Employment permit (back).

The following are notified of this decree:

1. Central commercial office in Bratislava.
2. District or (state police) office in Presov to institute control and to register under the permissible workers.
3. The Notary office in Presov to deliver this decree to the addressee 4-6 days after the assessed payment and the special levy was paid and an 8 Ks stamp was affixed.
4. Lignum lumber mfg, the petitioner and employer of the Jew.
5. Jozef Kornfeld, residing in Kapisova the employed Jew.
6. The Gendarme station (or state police office) in Presov.

for the accuracy of the
script control chairman
[Signature]

On guard!
For the minister
Dr. **Konka** signed

Identity card used by Jozef Kornfeld with Ludovit Argay's name.

Proof of Identity

Name: Argay Ludovit
Birth date. 23.VIII.1917
Birth place. Hatalov
Religion: Rom. Cat.
Profession: Wood processor
Residence: Svaty Jur
Height: tall Face: oval
Hair: chestnut brown Eyes, gray-green
Nose: normal Mouth: round
Special marks: .-.
2.X.1943
[Stamp] District Notary Office in Svaty Jur.

(The missing picture was used for Jozef Kornfeld's German passport on March 22, 1945.)

PERSONENBESCHREIBUNG

Staatsangehörigkeit: Slowakei
Beruf: Hilfsarbeiter
Geburtsort: Hatalov
Geburtstag: 23.8.1917
Wohnsitz oder Aufenthaltsort: Haunstetten Ldkrs. Augsburg
Gestalt: 1,81 m
Gesicht: oval
Farbe der Augen: braun
Farbe des Haares: dunkelblond
Besondere Kennzeichen: keine

Nr. 24619 2J/44

Unterschrift des Inhabers
Argay Ludovit

Nr. 24619 2J/44

Permit to enter Messerschmitt buildings (front).

Temporary Note No. 4673

Mr. Argay Ludovit born. 23.8.17 end. 2.3.45
Mrs.
Miss

is authorized to enter the Building segment A, also Work place I a,c,d,II a,b.c.IV a.b
Valid up to 30 June 1945
Extended to ....
22.3.45 Work security
[Signature]

The temporary note is to be surrendered to the Work security right after expiration.

Permit to enter Messerschmitt buildings (back).

>Pst< The enemy is listening!

I am aware that over everything I will see or hear in connection with the company visit, I will absolutely keep Quiet and protect.

Signature

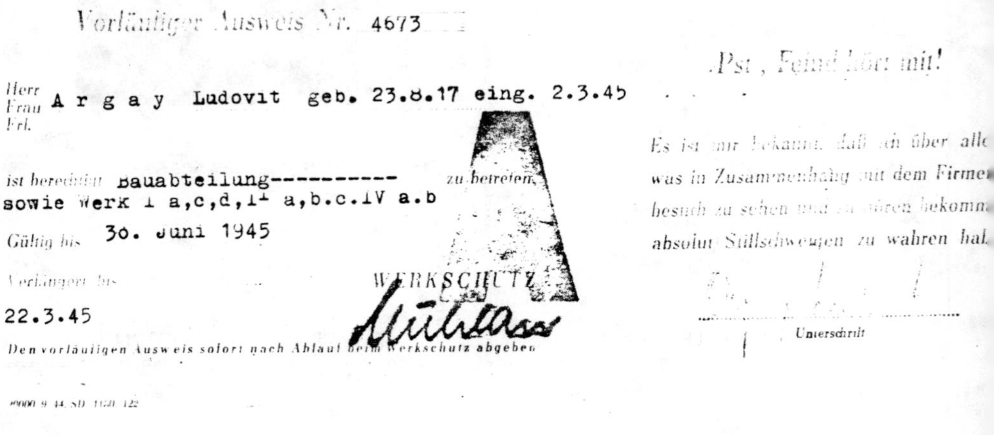

Vorläufiger Ausweis Nr. 4673

Herr
Frau A r g a y Ludovit geb. 23.8.17 eing. 2.3.45
Frl.

ist berechtigt Bauabteilung---------- zu betreten,
sowie Werk I a,c,d,II a,b.c.IV a.b

Gültig bis 30. Juni 1945

Verlängert bis ....

22.3.45 WERKSCHUTZ

Den vorläufigen Ausweis sofort nach Ablauf beim Werkschutz abgeben

Pst, Feind hört mit!

Es ist mir bekannt, daß ich über alle was in Zusammenhang mit dem Firmenbesuch zu sehen und zu hören bekomm absolut Stillschweigen zu wahren hab

Unterschrift

Permit for trip to Munich

Factory Augsburg **Office Trip-Order**

Name Argay **Given name** Ludovit **Control No.** 4673 **Expense account No.** 1 844

Purpose of trip Discussion at the Slovak Consul

Firm, Authorities Consul

Place Munich

Travel Expenses to be charged to: Expense account No. 1 844

Date of Departure 19.3.45 **Anticipated travel time** **1 day** **Need Travel Funds RM** [Reichsmarks] 40

Date 17.3.45 **Department head** Treuer Section Director Travel Office

[Signature] [Signature]

Travel accounting on the above official trip

Date	Train departure	from	to	Train arrival	Class	With or Without sleeper	RM	Pf.

Werk Augsburg	**Dienstreise-Antrag**	Beleg-Nr.	
Name: A r g a y	Vorname: Ludovit	Kontroll-Nr. 17673	Kostenstelle Nr. 1 844
Reisezweck: Rücksprache beim slowakischen Konsulat			
Firmen, Behörden: Konsulat			
Orte: M ü n c h e n			
Die Reisekosten gehen zu Lasten: Kostenstelle Nr. 1 844	Verkaufs-Auftrags-Nr.	Betriebs-Auftrags-Nr.	
Abreise Datum 19.3.45	Voraussichtliche Reisedauer 1 Tage	Benötigter Reisevorschuß RM 40	Spesen-Klasse verh./ledig
Datum 17.3.45	Abteilungsleiter [signature]	Zuständige Direktion [signature]	Reisebüro [signature]

Überschneidet sich die Dienstreise mit Flak- oder Luftschutzdienst? Ja/Nein. Verantwortlich: Abteilungsleiter

Spesenabrechnung zur obigen Dienstreise

Datum	Zug-Abfahrt	von	nach	Zug-Ankunft	Klasse	mit/ohne Schlafwagen	RM	Pfg.

Zu buchen auf Konto		RM	Pfg.
	Tagegelder mit/ohne Übernachten je RM Inland		
	Tagegelder mit/ohne Übernachten je RM Inland		
	Übernachtungsgelder je RM Inland		
	Tagegelder mit/ohne Übernachten je RM Inland/Ausland		
Gebucht	Tagegelder mit/ohne Übernachten je RM Inland/Ausland		
	Übernachtungsgelder je RM Ausland		
	Sonstige Aufwendungen nach anliegenden Belegen und umseitiger Aufstellung.		
	Summe der Spesen		

RM ______ in Worten ______ /100
erhalten.

Ort ______ Datum ______ Unterschrift ______

	Abgerechnet	Geprüft Abteilungsleiter	Geprüft Reisebüro	Angewiesen Reisebüro
Name				
Datum				

30000. 2. 45. SD. 1130. 4721

Travel permit. (Security was so tight that it was not possible to enter a railroad station to buy a train ticket without a travel permit.)

German Reich train
Presidium of the Reich train-
transportation office
Augsburg

Augsburg, date 23 Mar 1945

Travel Permit

Mr. Mrs. Miss Ludovit Argay
is authorized to travel from 23.03 to 23.04
from Augsburg Main station
via Munich, Vienna, Bratislava
and Zilina and return.

[Signature]

This verification authorizes the purchase of travel tickets only for the above mentioned trip and only upon presentation with a clear pictured I.D. He is to present at the time of the ticket purchase his travel permit. Also by entering the station and during the ticket control on the train and upon any request.
Every misuse will have punishable consequences.

Deutsche Reichsbahn
Der Vorstand des Reichsbahn-Verkehrsamts
Augsburg

Augsburg, den 23. März 1945

Reisegenehmigung

Herr – Frau – Fräulein ....
ist berechtigt in der Zeit vom 23.03. ....bis 23.04.......
von Augsburg Hbf. ....
nach ....u.zurück zu reisen.

23. MRZ. 1945

Diese Bescheinigung berechtigt zum Lösen von Fahrkarten nur für die angegebene Reise und gilt nur in Verbindung mit einem Lichtbildausweis. Sie ist bei Lösung der Fahrausweise, an der Bahnsteigsperre, bei der Fahrkartenprüfung im Zuge und auch auf Verlangen vorzuzeigen.
Jeder Mißbrauch wird strafrechtlich verfolgt.

Letter of introduction from Messerschmitt to the Slovak Consul

To the Slovak Consul
Vienna

21.3.45

Subject:

The one by us employed Slovak citizen

Argay Ludovit

is commissioned by us to undertake a discussion with you if there exists a possibility to send 3 to 4 people to Bratislava.

The people should try there for 400 Slovak workers who are here engaged by the Messerschmitt A.G. to secure clothing, shoes and bedding.

Since the consul is not any more in Munich, but in Vienna and the distance from Vienna to Bratislava is about 30 to 35 km, hence we issued a travel order direct to Bratislava, because it would be unwise for the people, after granting them a Visa to return to Augsburg and then again take the trip to Bratislava.

We are asking you to be very supportive to Mr. Argay in his undertakings and be helpful to him in every way possible so he can accomplish this order.

Mr. Argay undertook the responsibility for himself and the people accompanying him to return the shortest way possible, after finishing the mission.

Heil Hitler
Messerschmitt A.G.
[Signatures]

MESSERSCHMITT A.G.

MESSERSCHMITT A.G. · AUGSBURG

An das
Slowakische Konsulat

W ie n
======

AUFSICHTSRAT: THEO CRONEISS, VORSITZER
F. W. SEILER, STELLV. VORS.
VORSTAND: WILLY MESSERSCHMITT, VORSITZER
FRITZ H. HENTZEN, RAKAN KOKOTHAKI
BANKEN: BAYER. VEREINSBANK, FILIALE AUGSBURG
DEUTSCHE BANK, FILIALE AUGSBURG
BANKHAUS F. W. SEILER & CO., MÜNCHEN
GIROKONTO NR. 68/819
BEI DER REICHSBANKSTELLE AUGSBURG
POSTSCHECK: NR. 19873 BEIM POSTSCHECKAMT MÜNCHEN
FERNRUF: 8251
DRAHTANSCHR.: MEFLUG AUGSBURG
FERNSCHREIBER: K 6338

Ihre Zeichen | Ihre Nachricht vom | Unsere Zeichen WAE-H/AE/Tr/Ma (bei der Antwort bitte angeben) | AUGSBURG, den 21. 3. 45

Betrifft:

Der bei uns beschäftigte slowakische staatsangehörige

A r g a y   Ludovit

ist von uns beauftragt mit Ihnen Rücksprache zu nehmen ob die Möglichkeit besteht 3 bis 4 Leute nach Pressburg zu schicken.

Die Leute sollen dort versuchen für 400 slowakische Arbeiter die hier eingesetzt sind bei der Messerschmitt AG. Bekleidungsstücke, Schuhe und Wäsche zu besorgen.

Das das Konsulat nicht mehr in München sondern in Wien ist und die Entfernung von Wien nach Pressburg nur ungefähr 30 bis 35 km ist, haben wir die Leute gleich mit einem Fahrtausweis nach Pressburg versehen, da es widersinnig wäre die Leute nach Erteilung eines Visums erst wieder nach Augsburg und dann wieder nach Pressburg in Marsch zu setzen.

Wir bitten Sie Herrn Argay bei seinen Bemühungen unterstützen zu wollen und ihm zur Durchführung seines Auftrages behilflich zu sein.
Herr Argay hat für sich und seine Begleiter die Verpflichtung übernommen, nach Erledigung des Auftrages auf dem kürzesten Wege wieder zurückzukommen.

Heil Hitler!

M E S S E R S C H M I T T A.G.

i.A. [signature]   i.A. [signature]

		Bearbeiter	Apparat
		Treuer	625

Me 00073. 1. 42. 100000. 0/1396

Leave of absence permit (front).

Leave of Absence Permit
No. 4199807

The: Ludovit Argay
From: Hatalov (Slovakia)
born: 23.8.17 employed as: Worker
is from 23.3.45 to 12.4.45 to Bratislava and Zilina furloughed
Purpose of furlough: official trip to negotiate nourishment matters.
The furlougher is with a return travel ticket---equipped.
The furlougher was properly informed of the currency regulation and how much he can carry with him in domestic and foreign currency.
The furlougher is obliged after the end of his furlough to return to his work place. He is in Germany by the gen. local health insurance district office in Augsburg insured.

Augsburg: the 22.3.1945 [Company seal & signature]

Leave of Absence permit (back).

Verification of the Works office
Augsburg

The permission to one way travel from the country and reentry is conceded.

Augsburg, the 22.3.45

(Works office No. 3 Augsburg official stamp)

On order
[Signature]

Note of the Works office or the transportation stab for German works front over the usage of the train:

Rules usages is allowed.

The German Works front
[Signature]

...übertritt ist nur unter Vorlage eines gültigen Passes (Paß-
...apiers) und eines gültigen Sichtvermerks zur Ausreise und
...ereinreise gestattet. Der Urlaubsschein ist mitzuführen und
...s zur Beendigung der Urlaubsreise sorgfältig aufzubewahren.

Urlaubsschein

Nr. 4199807 *

Der/Die ...cvit (Vorname) Argay (Familienname)

aus Hatalov (Slowakei) (Heimatland, Heimatort)

geb. am 23.8.17., beschäftigt als Arbeiter

ist vom 23.3.45 bis 12.4.45 nach Preßburg-Sillein

... Sillein (Urlaubsort) beurlaubt.

Grund des Urlaubs: Dienstreise zur Regelung von Unterhaltsangelegenheiten (Familienheimfahrt, Krankheitsurlaub, Heimaturlaub, besondere Anlässe usw.)

Der Urlauber wird mit Rückfahrkarte bis ---- abgefertigt.

Der Urlauber ist über die für die Mitnahme von Geldmitteln in deutscher und der betreffenden ausländischen Währung geltenden Bestimmungen unterrichtet worden.

Der Urlauber ist verpflichtet, nach Beendigung des Urlaubs die Arbeit in unserem Betrieb wiederaufzunehmen. Er ist in Deutschland bei der Allg. Orts- Krankenkasse — Bezirksknappschaft — in Augsburg versichert.

Augsburg, den 22.3. 1945. MESSERSCHMITT A.G.

(Firmenstempel und Unterschrift)

Bescheinigung*) der Krankenkasse

— Bezirksknappschaft — in

Der Beurlaubung de..... kranken — schwangeren — Versicherten nach (Land)

wird ... zugestimmt.

..., den ... 194

(Dienststempel) (Unterschrift der Krankenkasse oder Bezirksknappschaft)

Auf dem Schein darf nicht radiert oder verbessert werden.

*) Nur im Falle der Beurlaubung einer erkrankten oder schwangeren Arbeitskraft auszufüllen.

Wenden!

A 226 (3.43) Reichsdruckerei 20150 43 9 0

Bescheinigung des Arbeitsamts

Augsburg

Der Erteilung des Sichtvermerks zur einmaligen Ausreise und Wiedereinreise wird zugestimmt.

Augsburg, den 22.3.45 194

Im Auftrag

(Dienststempel) (Unterschrift)

Vermerk des Arbeitsamts oder des Transportstabes der Deutschen Arbeitsfront über den zu benutzenden Zug

Regelzug-Benützung wird bewilligt

(Stempel)

Krautwurst

Official Trip Order.

Factory Augsburg

Official Trip Order

Name	**Surname**	**Control No.**	**Charge to.**
Argay	Ludovit	4673	1844

Purpose of Trip
Official travel to the Slovak consul to Vienna-Bratislava-Zilina.

Firms, Authorities
Consul

Place
Munich-Vienna-Bratislava-Zilina

Travel expenses to be charged to: Cost account 1844

Date of departure	**Anticipated travel time**	**Needed travel funds**
23.3.45	21 days	RM 100.--

Dated	**Department head**	**Section Department**
21.3.45	Treuer	[Signature]

Travel accounting on the above official trip

Ueb. rschneidet sich . . Dienstre. . mit Volk sturm, Flak- oder Luftschutzdienst? Ja/Nein.

Werk Augsburg — **Dienstreise-Antrag** — Beleg-Nr.

Name A r g a y — Zuname Ludovit — Kontroll-Nr. 4673 — Kostenstelle Nr. 1844

Reisezweck Dienstreise z. slowakischen Konsulat nach Wien-Pressburg-Sillein.

Firmen, Behörden Konsulat

Orte München-Wien-Pressburg-Sillein.

Die Reisekosten gehen zu Lasten: Kostenstelle Nr. 1844 — Verkaufs-Auftrags-Nr. — Betriebs-Auftrags-Nr.

Abreise Datum 23.3.45 — Voraussichtliche Reisedauer 21 Tage — Benötigter Reisevorschuß RM 100.-- — Spesen-Klasse — verh./ledig

Datum 21.3.45 — Abteilungsleiter Treuer — Zuständige Direktion [Signature] — Reisebüro

Spesenabrechnung zur obigen Dienstreise

Datum	Zug-Abfahrt	von	nach	Zug-Ankunft	Klasse	mit/ohne Schlafwagen	RM	Pfg.

Zu buchen auf Konto

Gebucht

Tagegelder mit/ohne Übernachten je RM Inland	
Tagegelder mit/ohne Übernachten je RM Inland	
Übernachtungsgelder je RM Inland	
Tagegelder mit/ohne Übernachten je RM Inland/Ausland	
Tagegelder mit/ohne Übernachten je RM Inland/Ausland	
Übernachtungsgelder je RM Ausland	
Sonstige Aufwendungen nach anliegenden Belegen und umseitiger Aufstellung.	
Summe der Spesen	

RM ______ in Worten ______ /100 erhalten.

Ort ______ Datum ______ Unterschrift ______

	Abgerechnet	Geprüft Abteilungsleiter	Geprüft Reisebüro	Angewiesen Reisebüro
Name				
Datum				

20 000. 2. 45. SD. 1130. 472/2

Authorization for five workers to undertake mission. (For Joe and his comrades, this was the most important mission-related document.)

<u>Certification</u>

Subject:

The Slovak Citizens
- Argay Ludovit...
- Bednarik Josef...
- Luptak, Matej...
- Longauer Jan...
- Potaucok Pavel...

are on an official trip for the Company Messerschmitt A.G. from Augsburg through Munich, Vienna to Bratislava, Zilina and return.

The authorities are being asked, since it is a matter of an important official mission, to support the above mentioned in their endeavor to accomplish their task.

Messerschmitt AG
[Signatures]

MESSERSCHMITT A.G.

MESSERSCHMITT A.G. AUGSBURG

BANKEN: BAYER. VEREINSBANK FILIALE AUGSBURG
DEUTSCHE BANK FILIALE AUGSBURG
BANKHAUS F. W. SEILER & CO., MÜNCHEN
GIROKONTO NR. 661.19
B. DER REICHSBANKSTELLE AUGSBURG
POSTSCHECK: NR. 19673 BEIM POSTSCHECKAMT MÜNCHEN
FERNRUF: 8231
TELEGRAMM: MEFLUG AUGSBURG
FERNSCHREIBER: 5 671 4
REICHSBETRIEBS-NR.: 0/0836/0006

B e s c h e i n i g u n g
==================================

AUGSBURG

WAE-H/AE/Tr/Na

Betrifft:

21.3.45

Die slowakischen Staatsangehörigen

Argay Ludovit,	Kontr.Nr.	4573,	geb.	23.8.17
Beduarik Josef,"	"	4454.	"	29.3.17
Luptak Matej,	"	3843.	"	13.3.13
Longauer Jan.	"	3865,	"	26.9.96
Potaucok Pavel."	"	----	"	10.1.13

befinden sich auf der Dienstreise für die Firma Messerschmitt AG., von Augsburg über München, Wien nach Pressburg-Sillein und zurück.

Die Behörden werden gebeten, da es sich um einen wichtigen Dienstauftrag handelt, die Vorgenannten bei Durchführung ihres Auftrages zu unterstützen.

M E S S E R S C H M I T T AG
i.A.

		Treuer 625

Official Confirmation of and request for funds for the trip to Bratislava and Zilina.

Confirmation

over the right of exiting and entering of currency on grounds of general business travel undertakings, established on grounds of
RE 27/43D. St. of the Reich's economy ministry of 22 June 1943

This confirmation serves the legitimacy towards the German custom officers at border crossings: it is **not** to be used to enrich oneself with foreign currency.

The interpreter Ludovit Argay travels on
(Accurate description) (Given name) (Surname)
orders of the Firm Messerschmitt A.G. Augsburg to: Bratislava-Zilina.
On grounds of the company's general allowances for Business expenses No. C IV 5021/45 of 5.1.1945 he is entitled:
2. the following mentioned foreign cash currency to exit with and with the unused sums to return.

Sum and Currency	Sum in Words
Ks 3000	Three thousand Slovak Crowns

This permit looses validity after three months from the issuing time.

The Chief Finance Officer Munich 23.3.1945
(Foreign currency dep.)
[Signature]

Bestätigung

über die Berechtigung zur Ausfuhr und Wiedereinfuhr von Zahlungsmitteln auf Grund einer Allgemeinen Geschäftsreisegenehmigung, ausgestellt auf Grund des RE 27/43 D. St. des Reichswirtschaftsministers vom 22. Juni 1943

Diese Bestätigung dient lediglich zur Legitimation gegenüber den deutschen Zollbeamten beim Grenzübertritt; sie berechtigt nicht zum Erwerb von Devisen

Der Dolmetscher (genaue Berufsbezeichnung) Ludovit (Vorname) Argay (Zuname)

reist im Auftrage der Firma Messerschmitt AG., Augsburg

nach Preßburg-Sillein

Auf Grund der seiner Firma erteilten Allgemeinen Genehmigung für Geschäftsreisekosten Nr. C IV 5021/45 vom 5.1. 1945 ist er berechtigt,

1. nachstehend aufgeführte Reiseschecke — Kreditbriefe — Akkreditive auszuführen:

Land	Art der Zahlungsmittel und Betrag

2. nachstehend aufgeführte **bare ausländische Zahlungsmittel oder Reichskreditkassenscheine** auszuführen und nichtverbrauchte Beträge wieder einzuführen:

Betrag und Währung	Betrag in Buchstaben
Ks 3000.--	(Dreitausend slowak. Kronen)
	( )
	( )

3. über die Reisefreigrenze von 10 RM hinaus weitere 50 RM in **deutschen Scheidemünzen oder Rentenbankscheinen** (auf keinen Fall Reichsmarknoten!) aus- und wiedereinzuführen. Die Mitführung dieses Betrages während der Auslandsreise soll eine Hinterlegung an der Grenze bei der Ausreise überflüssig machen und den Reisenden in den Stand setzen, bei der Wiedereinreise Ausgaben ab Grenze bis zum Eintreffen im inländischen Wohnort zu bestreiten; eine Verwendung oder Umwechslung im Ausland ist verboten. Für höhere Beträge empfiehlt sich die genehmigungsfrei zugelassene Mitnahme von Postreiseschecks, Postsparbüchern oder Kreditbriefen, die der Inhaber nur im Inlande einlösen darf. Im Rahmen der Reisefreigrenze von 10 RM ist auch der Erwerb und die Mitnahme ausländischer Zahlungsmittel gegen Paßeintragung statthaft.

Da die Bestätigung zur Aus- und Wiedereinfuhr dient, ist sie von dem Reisenden bis zur Wiedereinreise in das Reichsgebiet sorgfältig aufzubewahren und alsdann ohne Aufforderung an den deutschen Zollbeamten abzugeben.

Die Bestätigung tritt drei Monate nach ihrer Ausstellung außer Kraft.

Stempel

München, den 23.3. 1945

Der Oberfinanzpräsident München (Devisenstelle)

(Unterschrift der Devisenstelle)

Vordruck Dev. V 1 Nr. 10

Gr. A und B Berlin

8499 43 2 C